ISBN: 978129012609

Published by:
HardPress Publishing
8345 NW 66TH ST #2561
MIAMI FL 33166-2626

Email: info@hardpress.net
Web: http://www.hardpress.net

Mowbray's Devotional Library

EDITED BY
B. W. RANDOLPH, D.D.
Principal of Ely Theological College, and Hon. Canon of Ely

Savonarola

[After Fra Bartolommeo]

Spiritual and Ascetic Letters of Savonarola

EDITED BY
B. W. RANDOLPH, D.D.

WITH A FOREWORD BY
HENRY SCOTT HOLLAND, D.D.
Canon and Precentor of S. Paul's Cathedral

A. R. MOWBRAY & CO. Limited
London : 34 Great Castle Street, Oxford Circus, W.
Oxford : 106 S. Aldate's Street
New York : Thomas Whittaker, 2 and 3 Bible House

Preface

GIROLAMO SAVONAROLA was born at Ferrara, September 21st, 1452. His grandfather, Michele Savonarola, was a celebrated Paduan physician, and Girolamo was destined by his parents for the same profession. From quite early years he loved study and mysticism, and turned his back upon a worldly and pleasure-loving life. When he was nineteen, however, he fell in love with a girl of the proud Florentine family of the Strozzi, but his suit being refused he was thrown back upon himself, and for two years he remained in doubt whether to go on with his medical career or to devote himself to the direct service of God.

" Lord, teach me," he prayed daily, " the way in which my soul should walk." In 1474, through a sermon heard at Faenza, his prayer was answered, and his way made clear. Stealing away to Bologna in secret he entered a Dominican monastery, and from there he wrote to tell his father of the step which he had taken, and the reasons which had induced him to leave the world.[1]

In the monastery, in spite of his desire to do only menial service, his intellectual abilities were recognized, and he was made, after his profession, instructor of the novices.

It was not till 1482, in the thirty-first year of his age, that he was sent to San Marco, in Florence, a place henceforth for ever sacred to his memory.

Florence was at that time dominated by the influence of Lorenzo the Magnificent— and the Florentines were " dazzled by his splendour and devoted to pleasure and luxury." Ribald songs rang through the streets, and all true appreciation of morality and religion seemed to have disappeared from men's lives.

Savonarola in his first Lenten course at San Lorenzo in 1483 attracted few hearers, but two years later in a sermon on the Apocalypse, at Brescia, he made an ineffaceable impression on his contemporaries by his threats of wrath to come as well as by the tender pathos of his assurance of the divine mercy for the penitent.

On his return to Florence in 1491, his fame as a preacher had anticipated him.

[1] That letter is the first in the present collection.

The garden at the convent at San Marco was too small for his audience, and he preached his first sermon in the church attached to the monastery.

Next year he preached in the cathedral, and from that occasion his ascendancy over Florence began.

Lorenzo tried in vain to silence the stern preacher, or to induce him to moderate his violent denunciations, but it was of no avail. "Tell your master," he said to the messengers whom Lorenzo sent to him, "that albeit I am a humble stranger and he the lord of Florence, yet I shall remain and he shall depart."

Lorenzo died the next year, Savonarola leaving him unabsolved on his deathbed; and a few months later came the death of Innocent VIII, when the election of Cardinal Borgia to the Holy See brought the moral degradation of the Church to its lowest depths.

Meanwhile Savonarola's preaching became increasingly vehement. He saw visions and dreamed dreams. During one of his Advent sermons in the Duomo he beheld in vision a hand holding out a flaming sword inscribed with the words *Gladius Domini supra terram cito et velociter.*

He heard voices proclaiming God's mercy
on the good, His vengeance on the guilty,
and he saw, as he thought, the sword bent
towards the earth, "the sky darkened,
thunder pealed, lightning flashed, and the
whole world was wasted by famine, blood-
shed, and pestilence."

Meanwhile political changes made
Savonarola the lawgiver and chief ruler
of Florence, for so (without holding any
official post) he practically became. By
his daily sermons he stirred the people up
to an extraordinary pitch of religious
emotion. The aspect of life, the appear-
ance of the streets, became completely
changed. Hymns and chants were sung
in place of low songs ; men and women
dressed plainly and abjured all worldly
vanities. People of all sorts — nobles,
scholars, artists — became monks. Even
the boys of Florence were organized into a
kind of sacred brigade, having for its object
the cultivation of a holy life. The city
was transformed into a Christian Republic,
owning Christ as its Head.

But such a state of things could hardly
last long, human nature being what it is.
Already Savonarola's enemies were plotting
his downfall. The prophet had never

scrupled to denounce the abuses of the
Papal Court, the immorality and nepotism
of the Popes, and now Alexander VI,
having seen a copy of Savonarola's reflec-
tions on himself, resolved to silence him.
First he tried methods of trickery ; a
Cardinal's hat was offered him, only to be
publicly rejected by the great preacher.
" No hat will I have," he cried from the
cathedral pulpit, "but that of a martyr
reddened with my own blood."

In 1495 a Papal Brief courteously
summoned him to Rome ; Savonarola as
courteously declined the invitation, and
later in the year he refused to obey a
second summons. A third followed, and
Florence was threatened with an interdict
in the event of another refusal. Savonarola
still resisted, and vainly strove to " reconcile
rebellion against the existing Pope with
fidelity to the Papal See."

But in 1497 the tide had turned against
him even in his own city. A magistracy
openly hostile to Savonarola was elected in
that year, and he was at the same time
excommunicated by a Papal Bull. He met
the sentence in characteristic fashion, by
declaring it null and void. He himself was
(so he held) divinely inspired, and the

immoral and simoniacally elected Alexander
Borgia was no true Pope. It was war to
the knife. Alexander, however, was the
stronger of the two. He had only to insist
and to wait. He sent Brief after Brief
bidding the Florentines either to silence
Savonarola or to send him to be judged at
Rome. At last Savonarola obeyed, and
he ceased to preach first in the Duomo
and then in San Marco ; but his obedience
came too late, popular passions were
aroused against him. A Franciscan friar
(Francesco di Puglia) challenged Savonarola to prove his doctrine by the ordeal of
fire. Savonarola himself treated the pro-
posal with contempt, but one of his disciples
foolishly accepted the challenge.

On April 7th, 1498, the Piazza della
Signoria was filled with an enormous crowd
to witness the barbarous ceremony. The
Dominicans, headed by Savonarola, were
on one side, the Franciscans on the other ;
but Fra Francesco did not appear ; delays
ensued ; excuse after excuse was put
forward by the Franciscans, and at last,
as a thunderstorm swept across the city,
the authorities declared that the ordeal
was clearly contrary to the will of God.
The enraged multitude, baulked of the

horrible sight they had anticipated, fell upon Savonarola and his followers, and it was only with difficulty that they reached San Marco in safety, Savonarola retiring to his cell, while the crowd in the square outside were clamouring for his blood.

The next morning the Signory decided on his arrest ; the monks and their friends shut themselves into the church, which was finally stormed. Savonarola, Fra Domenico, and Fra Silvertio, were taken away amid the execration of the populace and lodged in the Palazzo Vecchio.

Another Brief arrived from the Pope bidding the Florentines to send their victim to Rome. They did not do this, but they did what the Pope wanted. Savonarola was tried ; his judges being chosen from his bitter enemies. Day by day he was tortured, and under his terrible sufferings he made the admissions his tormentors demanded, only to repudiate them again when released from the rack and free from the delirium of pain.

A further mock trial was held by two commissioners of the Pope, the Papal orders being that Savonarola was to die, " even were he a second John the Baptist."

Accordingly, on May 22nd, 1498,

sentence of death was pronounced on himself and his two disciples. Savonarola was allowed an interview with these two on the night before the execution, and next morning they were led to the scaffold. First they were formally degraded, the priestly vestments being stripped off, but when the Bishop pronounced the sentence, "I separate thee from the Church militant and the Church triumphant," Savonarola exclaimed, "Not from the Church triumphant, that is beyond thy power."

His two companions were hung and burnt first, and then Savonarola himself.

So passed into eternity the man whose name will ever be revered as one who, amid the moral degradations of his time—a degradation which reached its climax in the scandalous lives of the Popes—stands forth as the fearless representative of true Christianity—as truly a saint and martyr as many whose names have found their way into the calendar of the Church.

The roll of great men contains few greater names than those of Fra Girolamo. Beneath the intellectual culture of the Renaissance Christians — and specially Christians in high places — seemed altogether dead to morality and religion.

Savonarola stands out at the end of the fifteenth century as the great prophet who dared to insist, in season and out of season, that there can be no true religion divorced from pure morals. It was for this that he suffered, for this that he was a true martyr.

———

The letters which are included in this little volume have been translated into English from the original, in most cases the Tuscan vernacular, for the first time by the Rev. Watkin Williams, Vicar of Monkton, near Ramsgate, and formerly Fellow of S. Augustine's College, Canterbury.

B. W. R.

THEOLOGICAL COLLEGE, ELY,
  Trinity Sunday, 1907.

b

Foreword

SAVONAROLA — the name leaps out of the page. There is that vitality in it which keeps it ever pregnant and personal. Every one seems to be aware of him as if he were an acquaintance, a friend. Interest quickens at the sound of the name, sure of having something that will concern it deeply. Only one or two men, who play a great part in some far-off history, possess this power of touching us with the intimacy of those who are near and dear : as if they were not dead memories of the historic past, but living companions who can never die.

He is one ; and Dante is another.

Is it something in the native force of these Mid-Italians, these men whom Florence either breeds or moulds ?

That Florentine air, so sharp and strong, seems to create a type of character that tingles, through and through, with the intensity of its personal *motif*. The individuality emerges into light, compact and entire, without the faintest film of

uncertainty to baffle our impression of it,
or to obscure or hinder its direct immediate
effect. Everything about it has distinction,
and originality, and character. The out-
lines are as clear and clean as the edge of
steel. Its passion is vivid and effective,
with the unhindered freedom of a flame.
There is no disguise : no veil : no travers-
ing medium : no distorting atmosphere :
no puzzling distance. Straight home, the
whole man tells on us, with the effectual
and ready swiftness of impress which
actual presence would, morally, give.
Nothing intervenes between us and him.
The curtain drops away. We feel him
near. We hear him speak. So marked,
so intense, so vital, are these creations
of wonderful Florence—Dante : Michel-
angelo : Savonarola.

I remember how an eager girl, on
her first visit to San Marco, found
Savonarola's cell filled with a party of
American tourists, talking in those strange,
harsh, unconcerned tones of theirs ; and
she burst into tears. It was to her a
personal desecration ; an outrage done to
a living man.

As with Dante, so with Savonarola, it
is the face which carries in it this peculiar

sense of intimate distinction. Who can ever forget it ? Who can escape its haunting fascination ? And the fascination lies in its vivid vitality.

It is far from beautiful. It may even shock by a certain commonness of grain, a certain violence of structure. It is the face of a man of the people ; it smacks of the soil. It has an elemental roughness in the strong lines of its features. This is the character of many of the Italian faces of that date. They look out at us from the delicate painting of the early Renaissance, with the direct simplicity which belongs to the face of a vigorous peasantry. The stuff of humanity is not sophisticated in these men. They have arrived straight at their work from the workshops of Nature. So with Savonarola's face. It is, above all things, real, undisguised, unmodified, emphatic. The man in him speaks through it. We are under his touch, in his grip. Here he is, present with us : and we are aware of it in every nerve of our being. His personality hammers at our souls. We are under the immediate sway of the restless and passionate eye, so strangely contrasted with the quiet control of the strong and intellectual mouth. Cover up the lower face, and you are in presence of the prophet : feverish, agitated, dangerous. Cover up the upper face, and you feel only the peace of assured self-mastery. The forehead is low, and wrinkled, and shrunken. The jaw is large, calm, powerful. You can see how difficult and how mixed were the materials that went to his making. Yet there is no uncertainty, or hesitation, or confusion in the immediacy with which all these cross-agencies are forced into the single jet of a self-identical personality. It is the face of one who goes straight forward, whatever happens, and who can fling into his personal presence the entire force of his undivided humanity.

So the face is with us, painted by the passionate love of those who owed their souls to him, through that swift and splendid tragedy of his. Every incident in it is known to us. It is instinct with dramatic effect from end to end. It moves on heroic lines always. It closes in a martyr-dom, clearly modelled on the type of the Cross of Christ. He deliberately sets himself to be as his Lord and Master, in his behaviour under the tyranny that did him to a like death.

And, ever and always, it was a passionate, personal voice that spoke through him to men's souls : and, ever and always, it was a passionate and personal devotion that he won from men's hearts. Love was the key of his being. Love spoke through all those strange expository sermons, with their scholastic pedantries, and their cramped contortions. Love, passionate personal love, broke through in outbursts as of flames through the bars of a furnace—love for Florence as for a bride ; love for Florentines as for brothers and sisters of his blood and of his love ; love for children, love for souls, love for God.

Such love as this will always speak with the same living force. Time can never make it stale.

And, therefore, I feel sure that it will find its way through the pages of this little book to many who would willingly draw nearer to the man whom they have always longed to know better.

Here, in these letters, we enter into his heart of hearts.

We see what his home was to him, in the letter to his father in excuse of leaving it. How real the letter is ! How young !

How full of the heroic exaggerations of youthful aspiration! How delightful in its youthful confidence in logic! The rhetoric is the rhetoric of romantic youth, at all times and in all places.

The other letters are harder to get inside : a little grim, perhaps, and very lengthy, and minute, and austere : but they reveal the love that found expression through the disciplined life, through the careful organization of the Brotherhood, through the Rule, and the Community, and the Order, and the cowl.

In all this he was a master-expert. And we may well take pains to arrive at the inner mind which made the Dominican Rule so dear to him.

The translator has given us a pleasant and favourable opportunity for studying the workings of a heart of fire in its innermost secret, when it outpours its intimate message to those who will understand.

He will be thanked by all who love the man of love—the man with the living soul —the man who for ever draws to himself the heart of all true lovers of the soul— Savonarola.

H. S. HOLLAND.

Amen Court, S. Paul's.

Contents

Contents

Spiritual and Ascetic
Letters of Savonarola

Letters of Savonarola

I

To his father, Nicolas Savonarola ; written at Bologna, 25 April, 1475 ; concerning his departure from home and his entrance into the Order of the Preaching Friars.

MY honoured father,—I doubt not at all that my departure hath been to you painful and distressing ; and I know it to have been the more distressing from the fact that I left you secretly and unknown to you.

Yet I would that by this letter my mind and intention may be fully revealed unto thee, that thus thou mayest be of a better courage and mayest understand that I was led unto the purpose in question by no means in that light and childish spirit as I hear is believed by many persons.

And, in the first place, this would I earnestly desire of thee, as of a manly character

B

which duly despiseth things that perish,
that thou wouldest regard and embrace
facts rather than, as poor women are wont
to do, mere feeling ; and that thou wouldest
judge, according to reason, whether it were
expedient for me to have left this world
and thus to hold fast by my purpose. For
this is indeed the chief reason which led
me to the Religious Life and to a monastery, namely, the boundless misery of this
world and the extreme unrighteousness of
most men, the adulteries, thefts, idolatries,
impurities and hideous blasphemies, unto
which this age hath so far reached that
there may be found none that doeth good.
For which cause was I wont ofttimes a day
to repeat with tears,
　　"Haste thee, haste to escape from a land
　　　　that is cruel and greedy."
And thus I did, because I was not able
to endure the utter iniquity of so many of
my fellow-countrymen : a state of things
which was, to my mind, the more serious
that I saw every virtue downtrodden and
crushed, and crime and vice promoted
and everywhere supreme ; for nothing hath
ever been more distressing to me than
this ; and accordingly daily did I pray the
more fervently unto the Lord Jesus Christ ;

and in order that God might take me out
of so great filth and uncleanness, with as
much devotion and earnestness of mind as
I could, was I wont continually to call upon
Him in this short prayer : "Show Thou
me, Lord, the way that I should walk in,
for I lift up my soul unto Thee."

Now hath God, in His own good time,
of His exceeding love towards me, at
length shown unto me a way into which,
unworthy though I be, I have entered and
on which I have held.   Now, I pray thee,
tell me : Is it not a fitting and glorious
work of virtue for a man to avoid the
defilements of this world ?   For a man to
live the life of reason and not, as do the
beasts, the life of sense ?   Moreover,
should I not rightly be held the most
foolish and the most ungrateful of men
thus vehemently to have prayed God that
He would open unto me right ways and
show unto me the path wherein I should
walk if, when He deigned so to do, I were
to turn away and wander from the path ?
O my Jesu, a thousand times rather may
I die than ever be guilty in Thy sight of so
deep an ingratitude !

Accordingly, most beloved father, thou
must not weep.   Nay, thou must render

unceasing thanks to the Lord Jesus in that
He hath granted unto thee a son and
those two-and-twenty years hath kept him
safe and sound. And, as though this
were not enough, He hath associated him
with Himself and chosen him to be His
own soldier. Ah, thou good sir, is it
not a distinction of grace, is it not a mark
of high favour that thou shouldest have
for thy son a knight who weareth the decora-
tion of Christ? Yes, indeed! But, most
beloved father, to put it in a word, either
thou dost love me or thou dost not.
Never wilt thou grant, I know full well,
that thou lovest me not. If, then, thou
dost love me, seeing that I consist, as do
other men, of soul and body, thou dost
prefer either the body to the soul or the
soul to the body; but, indeed, I may not
think nor suspect that thou lovest the body
rather than the soul, for truly to love me
were not, surely, to love my viler part.
But if thou dost truly love my soul, why is
it that thou dost not desire and seek after
my soul's good? Wherefore for this my
mighty victory won, for the very glory of
my triumph, it becometh thee with solemn
joy to keep high feast. Full well do I
understand that it can scarcely be that the

flesh should make nothing of what hath happened that it should not ill endure it, that it should not grieve ; but men of courage and of great heart, such as art thou, must subdue the flesh and control it by the exercise of reason. And dost thou not think that I too suffered most bitter anguish of mind in that it was right for me to be torn away from thee and separated from thee ?

Be assured that, indeed, never since the day that I was born, have I experienced more distressing or more violent anguish than that with which I was oppressed when, in the knowledge that I had been torn from my own father and my own flesh and blood, I found that I had gone away to a strange and unknown people, that I might sacrifice this body of mine to my Lord Jesus, and that I might freely place my entire self, my very will, in the power and authority of others, and that, as it were, sold at no price at all, I might deliver myself over into the hands of those whom I knew not. Yet thinking myself there-unto called by the Lord, Who willed even to be made man and to be humbled and to take upon Him the form of a slave, I could not but " incline my ear unto the

words of His mouth," and take heed unto
this His good and gracious message :
" Come unto Me, all ye that labour and
are heavy laden, and I will refresh you ;
take My yoke upon you."

Now, knowing, as I do, that ye have
been specially grieved and displeased that
I left you thus unbeknown to you, and that
I went away secretly like a fugitive, I pray
you to be assured that on my departure
I was so far overcome by sorrow, so far
affected by tenderness of heart, that, had
I beforehand made known to you my
purpose, I should have failed from excess
of grief before I had thought of leaving you,
my heart would have fainted within me,
and I should have become as one dead,
wholly beside myself, deprived of thought,
of feeling, of speech.   Spare, then, to
wonder and complain at my unwillingness
to be open with you, at my preferring
rather to leave on my departure a little
paper amongst my books at the window
that thus ye might be informed in the
matter.

I pray thee, therefore, most beloved
father, "let thine eyes cease from tears,"
and do not henceforth lament and grieve
over me even more than I do over myself,

—not indeed that I grieve as though I had done wrong, for were I greater and more distinguished than the Emperor, I should not suffer myself to be diverted even in the very least degree from my purpose, but simply that I am, as thou art thyself, still a man with fleshly appetite : and the flesh warreth against the spirit and the sense against the reason. Wherefore I have to undertake a bloody and a fearful contest, lest the devil prevail against me and that the more successfully in so far as thou art the nearer and the dearer unto me.

Soon, soon, believe me, will pass these thy days of bitterness ; with the flight of time a wound doth heal and fresh grief fadeth. Nay, moreover, I doubt not but that unto thee, even as unto myself, there will be vouchsafed consolation from the Most High, in this life through grace, in the life to come through glory.

Now, then, there remaineth this one thing which I would beg and pray of thee, namely, that thou as a man of courage and great heart wouldest do thine utmost to console and strengthen my mother, of whom and of thyself I do very earnestly beseech that ye would give me your parental blessing ; I, on my part, will constantly pray unto the Lord for the salvation and entire well-being of your souls.

Bologna, 25 April, 1475.
         JEROME SAVONAROLA,
                     Your Son.

Here I do commend unto thee all my brothers and sisters, and especially my brother Albert, for whose education I pray thee to take all possible care and precaution ; for it would be a terrible reproach and a sin unto thee, didst thou suffer him uselessly and idly to waste his time.

II

To Magdalen Pica, Countess of Mirandola ; concerning her design of entering the Order of S. Clare.

WHEN I learned, dearly beloved daughter in Christ, that having renounced the allurements of this world, thou wert with all thy heart longing after the true and eternal Spouse, the love of Christ, and, indeed, my own great regard for thyself and for thy family, constrained me to write unto thee a few words whereby thou mightest be strengthened in this thy purpose, and instructed in the ways of God and concerning that state of life of which, in the spirit of holiness, thou hast made choice, lest, perchance, in following in the footsteps of so many thou be also carried away by their error, even by the abuse of these days. For very many easily persuade themselves that they have renounced the world, which, as a matter of fact, they only exchange for a second world, leaving, as it were, one form of the world to enter into another : who, moreover, for the most part, by the craft of the

devil, in the end lose, as they say, both
worlds, failing to enjoy either the present
world or that which is to come.   Wherefore it is altogether necessary, most
beloved daughter in Christ, for any Religious thoroughly to understand the
purpose for which the monastery hath been
entered, and understanding forthwith to
meditate thereupon, and meditating thereupon to appreciate and to love it, and
loving it at length zealously to fulfil it.
For too many in these days have no
thought of why or wherefore they have
entered into Religion ; accordingly they
are neither able nor careful to reduce their
life to rule ; for the due consideration of
the end to be attained is the rule of all
human operations.   Some there are who,
although they do understand the end to be
attained, yet give thereto little or no attention and they live a life of idleness, doing
no worthy service in the cloister.   Others,
again, there are who, indeed, both understanding and giving heed to this their end,
yet failing to follow it and to esteem it with
adequate fervour of affection, are lukewarm
in God's cause and do His work with
scanty zeal, forgetful of the prophetic word,
" Cursed is the man who negligently

worketh the work of God." Certain others there are who even understand, give due heed to and rightly esteem this same end, but who, inasmuch as they work not with might and main, fall from their early zeal and most often lose the reward of the labours which they have endured.

Accordingly it is altogether thy duty and thy necessity, seeing that thou wouldest not endure to no purpose the hardships of the warfare thou undertakest, to have in clearest view that which is for all men the end of the Christian Religion, and especially for those who on account of the settled excellence of their lives are commonly called "Religious," taking, as it were, their title from their distinctive attribute,[1] it is, I say, thy duty and thy necessity to have this end in clearest view, ever to give it thy attention, to love it heartily, and zealously and unsparingly to labour to attain it. But although, in a certain sense, the latter and due end of the Christian is the eternal blessedness of the kingdom of heaven, yet, in this connexion, in speaking of the end, we mean not the latter end but the nearer end, unto which the godly Religious do unceasingly labour, and which

[1] *Religiosi* vulgo dicuntur *per Autonomasiam*.

is truly charity itself, the love of God and
of one's neighbour. For the saints and
the Religious strive earnestly, in spite of all
distraction, that their mind and soul may
be united by love and charity unto the
crucified Christ, and that they may attain
unto such union with Him as to exclaim
with the Apostle, "I am crucified with
Christ, nevertheless I live ; yet not I, but
Christ liveth in me."

Day and night, therefore, nought else
interesteth and occupieth their mind, nought
else their heart desireth or longeth after,
nought else doth their tongue tell of save
Christ Jesus and Him crucified ; so
possessed are they by love of Him that
for His sake no toil is heavy, no adversity
is bitter ; nay, they do count it honour and
hold it in high esteem if they are able to
suffer even in some small degree for His
sake Who for them deigned to die upon
the Cross ; so that, carried away by
that wonderful fervour of Paul, they are
able and bold to say, "But God forbid
that I should glory, save in the Cross of
our Lord Jesus Christ, by Whom the
world is crucified unto me, and I unto the
world." The soul's eye, then, of the true
Religious is ever seeking and regarding

this end and this love, and he holdeth himself to be growing or failing in Religion in proportion as this love groweth and increaseth or diminisheth in him, mindful of the Apostolic word, "Now the end of the commandment is charity out of a pure heart, and of a good conscience, and of faith unfeigned." Now, seeing that the perfection of this charity cannot be attained apart from purity of heart it is altogether necessary that he who would seek to have this divine love grow within himself should cleanse his heart from all earthly affection or carnal desire, and remove and utterly destroy the noxious spreading roots of his own will or sense, which either flourish naturally or grow from bad habits: for purity of heart indeed is the most important and the determining condition in effecting the love of Christ. For so soon as ever one hath abjured this world and hath cleansed his heart from every stain of sin, and hath purged it of corrupt affection for the creature, immediately there is abundantly shed abroad and increased in him the love of Christ Jesus crucified, the Eternal Spouse.

All men, then, should seek and should observe this purity and love ; and the

c

Religious, as we have said, should clearly understand that he hath entered into a monastery for no other purpose than that of cleansing his heart from earthly things and detaching it, and at length filling it entirely with the divine love. But seeing that it happeneth that from carelessness and inattention, a man sometimes turneth aside or wandereth from following after the end, therefore is it that he must ever have the end in full view of his eyes, that he must diligently consider it and give to it his attention, that he must follow after it and pursue it with all his heart, and finally, zealously, unwearyingly and unceasingly work it out.

And, indeed, this is the very purpose of the three vows of the Religious, namely, that all the stains of earthly and perishable things may be utterly removed from the heart. To begin with, the very vow of poverty, whereby the heart is cleansed from love of outward things ; not that it is sufficient to keep this vow merely in regard of outward things, but, rather, the spirit of poverty is in such sense to be cultivated as that the servant or the bride of Christ may desire to possess, even at the cost of toil and labour, only what is necessary for the bare sustenance of this life, placing no dependence upon man, but with full confidence in Jesus and the one God, Who alone nourisheth the whole universe.

Ah! my dearly beloved daughter, by how many in these days is this vow ill kept, who desire, indeed, to be poor in Religion after such a fashion that they may have all their needs supplied and may lack nothing! The greatness and refinement of the world they treat with rare disdain and will have none of them, and yet afterwards in Religion they entangle their hearts in the pettiest details, to wit, in the elegancies of the cloister, a smarter or a new tunic, a neater breviary, a wretched little knife or a pair of scissors, or any one of the two thousand such trifles, that for the most part hinder the peace and purity of the mind; and at length they come just to pass away the time in the monastery like some unproductive and unfruitful tree growing in a pleasure - garden. Oh! wretched lot of such, who have, indeed, cast far from them gold and silver, but blush not that thereafter they embrace the dust and mire!

Thou must, therefore, take due heed that as earthly spouses are wont to admire their beloved decked with gold and silver and fair with gems and pearls, so on the contrary, the Heavenly Spouse desireth and loveth His bride stripped of all earthly adornment and clothed only after that viler and poorer fashion which our present condition alloweth. For the poorer she be, alike in purpose and in effect, the more conformed is she, and thus the more acceptable, unto Himself.

We read concerning the elder Arsenius that, as, while a distinguished personage at the Imperial Court, no courtier was clothed more elegantly or more expensively than himself; so, afterwards, his state of life being changed, when he assumed the cowl, no hermit was more ragged; with the result that other monks, who in the world had been by many degrees his social inferiors, were ashamed now to be clothed better than was he. Indeed for all other devotees of the desert, he was pre-eminent as the true type and exemplar.

Do thou, therefore, my little daughter, who thinkest of abjuring earthly things, that thou mayest serve Christ, and of leaving the world that thou mayest follow Jesus, descend from thy state of wealth and dignity to the utter vileness and poverty of our Saviour Jesus Christ, and in the measure in which, wert thou in the world, thou wouldest outshine thine associates by thy possessions, by thy womanly grace or adornment, so, in Religion, seek to surpass them by outward vileness of attire and by inward humility of heart. For it becometh those who, while they followed the standard of the devil, strove to vanquish their own comrades, now that they have begun to take service under Christ, to surpass their fellows after such a fashion as this.

It will, therefore, be far from thee, and quite unseemly, to possess a new robe, or one of finer texture than the rest, or pretty little gilded books, or breviaries and other books which are works of art or have any value ; or anything, however useful and convenient, admirable for its beauty or its cost ; otherwise thou wouldest rightly be said not yet to have learned contempt of this world, but rather still to have in tender memory thine ancestral dignity and the base, vain things belonging to this evil day.

This is the manner of some who know little or nothing of the way of Christ ; for when they propose to betake themselves to a monastery they prepare for themselves new garments and innumerable things of the kind, which are not so much useless as unbecoming, in that they seem to be decking themselves to be brides, not of the poor and destitute Christ, but of this crooked generation.

Do thou, my spiritual daughter in Christ, avoid, I pray thee, these uses and abuses of the world; enter thy monastery in poverty and nakedness. See that thy habit be <u>coarse</u> and old, patched and stained; and whatsoever be altogether needful for thy life in the cloister let it both befit and savour of poverty and not vanity.

Let thy breviary be of no value, but roughly typed; not fine with the gold or vermilion of some skilful hand, beautiful with no silken latchets, no gilded tooling, lettering or other adornment; the title or the cross not of gold, but of leather or of yarn. Nay, if so it might be, it were far better for thee to possess no breviary at all of thine own, and to say the Divine Office either in company with others or, if need be, from memory; or, finally, to use a breviary assigned to the common use of the monastery or interchanged with thy fellows. Let thy books be clean and, although not ornamented, yet free from blemishes ; and, so soon as thou hast used them, restore them to the community. Let thy cell be so arranged as to be quite safely left open to all comers, even to thieves ; and let it contain nothing that is superfluous. Let thy bed be simple and humble, thy bookcase, thy little table ; in a word, let everything be suggestive of holy poverty.

Let there be in thy cell no image of the Infant Jesus, of carved or molten wax, which is a very idol of nuns in these days ; upon the worship and adornment of which they spend as much money as would relieve and enrich the state of many poor, for which indeed they will have to render account to God at the Last Judgment, to say nothing of the waste of time so uselessly spent upon these vain and childish things.

But thou must have thy crucifix, no part of it of gold or silver, nor finely wrought and finished, but rude and cheap, albeit of devout and godly spirit ; that thou mayest be moved to compassion and devotion, that thus thy petitions may be the more acceptable. Nor let thyself be so far deceived as to say, " My parents are great and wealthy ; it is a small matter or no matter at all for them to give me these valuables, these little gifts " ; for in a monastery thou must have no thought of the dignity of parents, but of the condition and poverty of that service of Christ which thou fulfillest ; so that it is thy business to take thought, not so much for thine own soul as for the example thou settest to others, and for their edification unto salvation, knowing for a surety in the sight of God that, in so far as thou dost cultivate this poverty and simplicity of life, thou dost make progress in purity and peace and love.

Nor, again, fall into the error of certain who hold that poverty consisteth not in an outward destitution of things, but in an inward lack of affection towards them. For although indeed this be true, yet it is agreed that it is most difficult, and scarcely possible, to possess those outward things, and not to be attached to them. For this reason the holy fathers of old time, although loving Christ unfeignedly, yet freely surrendered these things, thinking, thou must understand, earthly possessions to be the occasion of many a fault and sin.

And this is clearly and surely proved in the case of those Religious who, whether publicly in the community, or privately in their own cells, are rich in earthly things ; for they are lukewarm and even cold in love of Christ ; they are careless and inattentive in prayer ; they are sensual, talkative, complaining, passionate, impatient, greedy, uncertain, envious, idle, proud, and disobedient.   And this is their evil plight because they have departed from that great first principle of poverty, and they have altogether forgotten that he who would serve Christ in a monastery must be poor alike in inward purpose and in outward effect.

From this rule, which I have given thee, never suffer thyself to be seduced by the persuasion of any ; otherwise, believe me, nowhere, under any circumstances, wilt thou be content and tranquil.   Thus it is laid down by the teaching and authority of the holy fathers, thus is proved by the very experience of every day.

The second vow, by which the heart is cleansed from earthly and carnal affections, is the vow of chastity, which perfectly to keep how laborious and difficult

it is Augustine well showeth, saying :
" Amongst all the contests of the Christian the battle of chastity is alone severe,
in which there is daily warfare and rare
victory." But especially in youth is the
struggle toilsome, and the more difficult
in proportion as the aim is chastity both
of mind and body. But, seeing that there
be three special foes of chastity, namely,
the presence of external objects, the
prompting of the flesh, and the dangerous
thoughts that arise within the mind, the
holy doctors have devised and adopted
for the Religious a threefold shield and
sword wherewith to repel and slay this
three-headed enemy ; that is to say, the
seclusion of the cloister, austerity and
penance and, finally, continual exercise
both of mind and body ; and he who
neglecteth sedulously to avail himself of
these means cannot but fall in the contest and lose the victory.

But so far as the first of the means
is concerned, the seclusion of the cloister,
it is neither sufficient nor of any great
advantage unless within the monastery
itself the bride of Christ strive to live
alone and apart from others. For in
these latter times many are found shut

up within the enclosure of high walls who spend the whole day in conversation at the *grille* ; under pretence, indeed, of encouraging piety and devotion, they trifle and chatter with their friends or relatives and intimates, and invite and urge them to pay more frequent visits to the monastery ; whereas, were they in the least degree led by the Spirit, not only would they never wish to hear or see these people, but they would receive them a little more sternly, and send them about their business, in spite of their indignation or ill-will. Let them, then, read what beareth upon this point. Let them open the histories and the lives of the holy fathers, and let them learn that sons have denied themselves the visits of their mothers, brothers the visits of their sisters, and sisters the visits of their brothers, according to the word of the Lord : " I came not to send peace upon earth, but a sword. For I am come to set a man at variance against his father, and the daughter against her mother, and the daughter-in-law against her mother-in-law. And a man's foes shall be they of his own household."

Accordingly, dearest lady and little daughter in Christ Jesus, when thou enterest into a monastery send away from thee all thine own people, so that thou mayest wish, with regard to men especially, not only not to hear and see them, but not so much as to remember them any longer, obeying thus that invitation of the Eternal Father addressed to the bride of Christ Jesus, His dearly beloved Son : " Hearken, O daughter, and consider, incline thine ear : forget also thine own people and thy father's house. So shall the King have pleasure in thy beauty."

Be thou well advised and know for a surety that it is wellnigh altogether impossible to meet and to converse with secular persons, as is the habit of certain lukewarm and light-minded nuns, and at the same time to possess and to preserve an imagination free from vain or carnal desires.

But when thou shalt have been thus separated from the world, then, because of that perpetual warfare which is waged upon the spirit by the flesh, as it is said, "The flesh lusteth against the spirit, and the spirit against the flesh," thou must have another shield and javelin, that is to say, penance. In the matter of penance walk

thou in the middle course ; let not thy
penance be less or more than is right,
the exact measure of which is difficult
alike to judge and to observe ; nor is
there any sounder or better rule for tyros
and beginners than that which biddeth them
consult fathers who are masters of the
subject and have long been specially exercised in the way of perfection and in the
spiritual life.

Truly, it is fitting that the servant or
the handmaid of Christ should be ever
given to the practice of austerities, so
that there should always be little hardships in food and drink, in sleep and in
other necessaries of the body, of which
he maketh use as drugs and medicaments,
remembering in all things the word of
the Apostle, " your reasonable service."

Finally, there yet remaineth a third kind
of armour, that whereby we may resist the
onslaught of evil thoughts which attack us
on all sides, namely, continual exercise,
alike spiritual and bodily. To this end,
surely, it was of old ordained by holy
fathers that in a monastery the servants
of Christ should assiduously be occupied
either in spiritual exercises such as reading,
singing, meditation, and prayer ; or in bodily

D

exercises and manual labour. Whence Jerome saith, " See that thou always have some work in hand, that so the devil may find thee always busy." These three things if thou diligently observe thou shalt keep safe for Jesus Christ, Who is the spouse of thy choice, the flower of thy virginity and the lily of thy soul.

The third vow, the vow by which our heart is cleansed from disordered motions and affections of the spirit, is that of most holy obedience—obedience which excelleth all sacrifice and is far more acceptable than such in God's sight, as it is written, " Behold, to obey is better than sacrifice." Which obedience, if thou wilt promise and fulfil as becometh thee, being made like unto thy Spouse, Who "became obedient unto death, even the death of the Cross," thou must imitate a certain monk, who in a very short space of time attained unto a high degree of holiness. Entering into the monastery he said to himself, " Do thou and the ass be one ; be thou the kind of brother that the ass is." For the ass goeth wherever he is led, heavy burdens are laid upon him, he is beaten with the stick, and he holdeth his peace : so must thou, too, forget the empty glory of the world, of thy former and transitory state. And then thou must hold it deep in thy memory that we are all alike the children of Adam, born mortal and equal, that we all have one common lot and one common nature. Moreover, thou must call to mind the humility of our Saviour Christ, Who, although He were God, yet "emptied Himself and took upon Him the form of a servant," and of His free accord submitted Himself to the wills of most holy Mary and Joseph her husband, and was obedient unto them, in order that thenceforward, for His sake, it should be no shame for man to submit himself to his fellow. When, therefore, thou enterest into a monastery thou must know that thou doest so in order, not to be ministered unto, but to minister ; in order to obey and not to command ; and, too, in order to be subordinate to and obey such persons as, in the world, would have held it to be an honour and an advantage to have been able to minister unto thee.

Do thou, then, sincerely and resolutely set it before thyself to obey and to subject thyself, not only to superiors, but also to equals and to inferiors, " even as the Son of Man came not to be ministered unto, but to minister, and to give His life a ransom for many," remembering ever that His life was full on all sides of shame and lowliness, and that pride is the beginning and the root of all evils. Thus it was indeed that of old proud Lucifer fell headlong like a thunderbolt out of heaven, and the whole company of angels who followed him lost their good estate, "for whoso exalteth himself shall be abased, and he that humbleth himself shall be exalted."

And to put it in one word, when thou enterest into a monastery consider that thou knowest nothing either of good or evil save only what thou shalt have learnt therein ; contend with no one, neither at any time contradict or oppose any one, nor hold thyself to be wise, seeing that Christ our Saviour saith, "Except ye shall be converted, and become as little children, ye shall in no wise enter into the kingdom of heaven." Abide, then, humble in the monastery, like a little infant ; asking and ready to be taught, as one who did not enter thither in order to teach. For whatsoever Religious, especially if he be young, thinketh himself to be wise, turneth aside and wandereth from the way of God and of truth and knoweth not whither he goeth.

Let us return to what we spake of in the beginning. These three vows of Religion were instituted, we hold, in order to detach the mind from all love of the creature, in order to purify it both from carnal and outward affections, and from inward affections or self-esteem ; and in order that thus the heart, being cleansed and empty of self-esteem, may be filled with charity and wholly inflamed with love for Christ Jesus crucified, and at length may be made one with Him.

And, truly, all things which happen in Religion have been ordained with this end in view ; namely, fasts, vigils, solitude, silence, prayer, and the rest. The Religious whose mind is not continually fixed upon this end is unable to search and perceive what, if any, progress he is making in the Religious Life.

Accordingly we exhort thee, most beloved little daughter, whose desire is to be blessed both in this age and in the next, as thou hast already resolved, flee, I pray thee, and forsake this vain and deceitful world, and that not in measure nor by half, but totally and entirely, and transfer thyself wholly unto God, in love of Whom are found true peace and rest, as saith Augustine, "Thou, Lord, hast made us for Thyself, and restless is our heart until it find its rest in Thee"; moreover, diligently observing what we have already prescribed for thee, and strengthening thine observance by prayer, which is the chief study and business of the Religious.

But since there is no prayer but is the fruit of solitude and silence, the greatest care must be given to the restraint of the tongue; because, as saith the Apostle James, "he that thinketh himself to be religious and bridleth not his tongue, but deceiveth his own heart, this man's religion is vain." And, indeed, be assured that Religious are wont to be seduced by the devil by no means more easily than by the tongue; for under the pretence of recreation, or piety, or some other good thing, he leadeth them on to empty words, to endless chatter, often and again to backbiting, to evil-speaking, or to murmuring, regardless as they are of that saying of Solomon, "In the multitude of words there is sin." For the power of prayer, which before all else is a terror to the craft of the devil, is dissipated by much talking, and the Religious who is deprived thereof can nowhere scare that werwolf.

Although it be the duty of every Religious to bridle the tongue, it is especially becoming and necessary to the virgins of Christ so to do, for to them belong shamefacedness and modesty, to them belongeth when spoken to, but brief reply. Let their example be the Virgin Mother of God herself, who to the Angel of the Annunciation, proclaiming to her so many high and ineffable things, answered in a few short words just such as were necessary to give the angel her reply. Finally, by excess of speech the Religious loseth firmness and strength of mind, by it he disturbeth both himself and others.

Moreover, silence must have its companion, solitute ; nor will the one stand alone without the other, inasmuch as from both together there arise and are begotten, as it were of parents, elevation of mind and soaring unto God, as saith the Prophet, " It is good for a man that he bear the yoke in his youth. He sitteth alone and keepeth silence, because he hath laid it upon him."

Strive thou, therefore, in Religion to lead a solitary life and to be alone, especially at stated hours, and seek not to have requirements and friendships peculiar to thyself, but rather such as are common to thyself and others. Avoid, above all, the intercourse of companions who are wont to complain, or who live dissolutely, if such there be, and join thyself to those who live by the spirit and savour of the spirit, who are fragrant of the good odour of devotion, who are an example to their fellows ; who speak soberly, that is to say, at rare intervals and in measured terms ; whose presence and manner are not severe and pompous, but rather lowly ; from whom also thou mayest learn and appropriate some virtue ; and, as we have said, cultivate solitude and freely embrace it, solitude in which thou wilt feast and stimulate thy mind by the reading of sacred Scripture and of the holy doctors.

But my special advice to thee is that, next to the reading of Scripture, thou exercise thyself much in the reading of the Collations of John Cassian and of the fathers, and, in particular, of S. Jerome's edition of their Lives ; and meditate upon what thou hast read, and consider that the fathers have opened to thee a way in which thou mayest walk. But, after thy meditation, thou must lift up thy mind unto the Most High, thou must pray and beseech Him that He would deign to bestow upon thee the same graces and mercies as upon them, and that thou mayest have strength with all thy mind and with a heart pure, sincere and undivided, in adversity and in prosperity, unfailingly and faithfully to serve Him.

These things if thou shalt have duly fulfilled, then wilt thou ever be intent upon divine words. Moreover, thou wilt be able to observe the same rule in exterior exercises of the body; that is to say, let the hand be so given to labour as that the mind, too, may be occupied by spiritual things, and thus will He, thine Eternal Spouse, bestow upon thee the grace of contemplation, in which thou wilt taste and discern that which the world knoweth not, neither discerneth, and thou wilt pass thy days here below in joy and tranquillity; nor wilt thou have in thy life aught save what is grateful and, by the sweet love of Christ, thou wilt certainly not fail of the glory of the eternal kingdom; moreover, too, thou wilt pray God for me a sinner

that He would grant that with thee I also
may attain unto the triumph of that sub-
lime glory, Who is blessed for evermore.
Amen.

III

To his Brethren of the Convent of S. Mark at Florence; written at Bologna, where he was preaching during the Lent of 1492; concerning the manner of good living and of following after God.

BROTHER Jerome, by the mercy of God a servant of Jesus Christ, to his beloved young sons and to his brethren in Christ Jesus assembled together with one mind in the Convent of S. Mark at Florence : the grace of God and the peace of Jesus Christ be with you, my beloved young sons, from God the Father and our Lord Jesus Christ our Saviour, unto Whom I render thanks continually on your behalf because it hath pleased Him to grant unto you one heart and one mind in Christ Jesus, and a will prompt and devoted in His service, day and night interceding for you and praying that He would perform that good work which He hath begun in you, and that He would consummate it unto the confirmation in you of all virtues, so that ye may be as a burning lamp and a true light in the Church of

God, and as pillars to support His temple, which, as ye needs must see, tottereth even unto utter ruin.

Wherefore I beseech you, beloved, by the mercies of our Lord Jesus Christ, that ye fail not in the temptations and trials which threaten you, that ye be fully equipped, brave, duly trained, and strong to endure even greater hardships, and that, when the hour cometh, ye may be able, as gallant soldiers, to afford example and protection each one to his fellow. Accordingly ye must accustom yourselves to the endurance of continual interior temptation, and ye must strive manfully, in order that thus ye may possess the true tranquillity of mind, which is firmly rooted in the love of Christ and in the constant practice of virtue. For this is that one and unfeigned peace of mind "which passeth all understanding," which is gained by such spiritual warfare, and is neither the gift nor the possession of the world ; the peace of the world is enjoyed by many idle, inglorious, unwarlike souls, whose nature sleepeth in sloth, who do not war, and they, so long this peace lasteth, abstain from fighting. But that peace which is gotten by labour and spiritual conflict, standeth the firmer and the more severe, in so far as it can be shocked or disturbed by no alarms of war ; nay, it ariseth out of the very assaults of tribulation, it is established thereby, it findeth its strength and consolation in its own sufferings.

Wherefore, dearly beloved, seek diligently and give good heed to fight the good fight and play the man in order that ye may attain unto that peace which is the unsearchable treasure of man, that peace which they who have enjoyed have become partakers of the friendship of God, which the world cannot give, which is stronger than the world and more precious than the whole universe. Ah, dearly beloved, what do not poor worldlings suffer and endure in order that they may obtain that which they cannot keep for long, that which, compared with the happiness of Christian peace, is deserving of no account at all ? Therefore, dear sons, it is only as Christ illuminateth us that we can endure these things patiently, Christ, Who giveth peace and tranquillity to every one that asketh and worthily prepareth himself to receive them.

Although, indeed, "absent in the body,

E

yet I am present with you in the spirit "
and with all my heart will I endeavour
to aid you by my prayers to God, aye, and
to our Lord and Saviour Jesus Christ,
praying and interceding on your behalf
with Him and with His most holy Mother
Mary Ever-Virgin, and with our holy
patriarch Blessed Dominic, and the other
saints of our Order, but especially and
in particular with our most beloved and
tender father, the dearest of all patrons,
Bishop Antoninus, and with his companions,
that they would aid you and would deliver
you from the craft, fraud, and onset of the
enemy, and make you to abound in all
virtue and brotherly love, that ye may love
one another, supporting one another in
sincerity of heart, without dissimulation,
with all simplicity and gentleness, being
careful to preserve the unity of the Spirit
in the bond of peace ; holding yourselves
to be the least of all men, desiring rather to
minister than to be ministered unto, " in
honour preferring one another," as becometh faithful ministers of Christ. Lay-
ing aside every earthly and inordinate
affection, and with minds upraised to
heavenly things, at all times strive to lay
hold of that of which none can ever

deprive you against your will, and let all your confidence and consolation be found in the crucified Lord Jesus. Let your desire and your attention be set upon these words of our Lord and Saviour Jesus spoken unto Nicodemus : " God so loved the world, that He gave His only-begotten Son, that whosoever believeth on Him should not perish, but have eternal life."

Consider and weigh these words. Who is He that loveth ? God. Who is he that is loved ? The world, or all mankind, in misery and in sin. What is the pledge of love ? The Son of God, beloved and only-begotten. How is He given ? Hung upon a gibbet. Why, and for what end was He given ? To save us all from eternal condemnation and perdition, to bestow upon us all the gift of life. Finally, how small a thing is that which He desireth and asketh of us, namely, that we should believe on Him ! On Him, then, believe ye, beloved, and, believing, seek ye after Him through love. What shall I love more readily than the seeking after Christ, if there be in me the zeal of right living ? For we hold it as most certain fact, proved by long experience, that he liveth aright whosoever with whole and sincere heart loveth Christ crucified. Wherefore, as we have already often said, although the Christian Faith be most true and most assured, yet, were it possible for it to be in doubt or false, I should still desire to believe so long as I desired to live aright. Accordingly, to him that willeth and desireth it is not so hard and difficult a matter ; the gift of faith is ready to hand. For although it be the gift of God which is granted to whom He willeth yet we are able easily to prepare ourselves to obtain it and, when once it hath been granted and bestowed, to keep it upon the condition aforesaid. God, then, Who hath given unto us the Son of His love, hath in turn demanded of us very little, almost nothing ; faith, hope, and love which, if we are but in the least degree co-operating and pre- pared, He bestoweth upon us freely and without our merits. O truly inestimable gift of love ! O verily incomparable love ! May it, then, be now my care to take heed unto nought else, to have no thought or taste or love for aught else than these words of our Lord and Saviour which are unto my throat and heart "sweeter than honey and the honeycomb," which are unto me "above thousands of gold and silver," with which, in a word, no precious stone may be compared, but which are to be preferred before the wisdom of this world, before all kingdoms and dominions of the same. Recollect, therefore, day and night, dear sons, this word of the Lord, and it shall teach you the way of life, nay, indeed, by means of it shall every lovely thing in life grow sweet unto you. Pray unto the Lord, and earnestly desire of Him that He will reveal His law unto your heart, that He will make His light to shine upon you, that He will grant unto you to understand and apprehend these words of His, and, understanding them, to be wise thereby. Blessed are they who have been enlightened by the Lord! Many, indeed, vouchsafed but feeble ray, are wont to hear these words without partaking of them, and they are not strengthened thereby ; such persons stand in need of frequent meditation ; ye must ask the Lord that He will confirm and strengthen you in this word of His, that, too, ye may by study and diligent application attain unto a true understanding of the Holy Scriptures,

which indeed have no other purpose
than to lead men to a perfect knowledge
of the words which we have above recited;
and accordingly the Scriptures should be
read and re-read with frequent interest,
pondered with a pure mind in silence, in
unceasing prayer. Beloved, flee from
idleness, it is the parent and source of all
wickedness, for the suggestions of the
evil one are unto the idle. Beware of
the friendship and intercourse of secular
persons, even of relatives and of those of
your own family, especially of women,
though they be your very flesh and blood,
for moreover, "a man's enemies are they
of his own household." See that ye in-
dulge at no time in murmuring, vain and
idle words. When, therefore, ye meet
together let your words be seasoned with
grace, ministering to the edification, and
not to the confusion, of the hearers. Refrain from wandering from house to house,
lest ye become like fish perishing out of
water. Let the frequent and close occu-
pation of your own cells be unto you a
pleasure and delight; there let it be your
happy wont to read, to meditate, to pray,
and to contemplate. Persevere assiduously
in prayer. Remember that blind man

of whom next Sunday's Gospel tells us ; how instantly, unceasingly, perseveringly, although the crowd rebuked him and threatened him to be silent, yet the more did he cry unto Jesus that he might receive his bodily sight. Thus, following his example with a constant mind, do ye, too, persevere in prayer, seeking from Christ spiritual light. Nor, should the crowd of unreal things disturb you, be ye on that account deterred from prayer or shaken in mind, but pray ye then the more and the more fervently, for sure am I that if ye persevere in prayer, even as that blind man received from Christ the light of the body, so will ye obtain from the Lord that transcendent spiritual light whereby the ways of Christ may be opened unto you, and your life be founded in all spiritual joy and consolation.

I am ever mindful of your most sweet love, which is the subject of my frequent discourse with Brother Basil, my beloved son and partner in Christ Jesus, and your brother, who, with all earnestness, beggeth and urgeth me to tell you how warm is his love towards you, a love which burneth the more ardently that in these parts he findeth no such pleasant and gracious a com-

panionship as yours. Wherefore, like a
pair of turtle doves that wait for spring,
we both sit here solitary until we may
return to those warmer regions where we
are at home, and delight ourselves amidst
the perfumes of the flowers and the solem-
nities of the Holy Spirit. For although
there be found here not a few who are
intellectually pre-eminent, yet they use not
that simplicity which it is our wont to use,
to which simplicity, however, I would
feign think that by our intercourse very
many of them are easily to be recalled.
Give thanks, my dear brothers, to God
Who hath opened your inward eyes, and
hath prepared for you a way convenient
to the good and spiritual life. For here
darkness is everywhere spread, and many,
although they be brave and have a good
will, yet they follow not nor find the right
path upon which, perchance, some day
they may have the happiness to light
according to the measure of their zeal
and of their desire of advancing in the
way of God.

Dearly beloved, see that ye be not at
all backward or lukewarm, lest perhaps
there arise a new generation and it surpass
you ; let this saying of Christ be fulfilled

in you, "The first shall be last, and the last first." For already certain, with their loins girt and their lamps burning, have come to me, seeking direction, although they have not yet heard my voice here, while to you I have often spoken many things, both in private and in public. How great, I pray you, would be your condemnation were ye to allow yourselves to be forestalled and surpassed by these "last"? Ever and anon recall to mind my words of warning. Unless I be hindered and something grave prevent me, I will write unto you every week, so that, although I be absent, ye may receive the little word of exhortation which ye are wont to receive from me face to face; I shall, however, be compelled to put it in brief, that I neglect not my preaching and my study. It will, then, suffice that I remind you of those things which ye have so often heard from me by word of mouth.

I know that my departure was a sorrow to you, but the Lord hath dealt mercifully with you, Whose will is that ye should hope unto the end lest ye should be overtaken by a keener or a premature sorrow. Now, therefore, dear brothers, detach yourselves from all human affection,

aye, even from your affection for myself.
For it is written, "Cursed is he who
trusteth in man." Although truly ye love
me with no carnal but with spiritual affection, nor for the sake of any temporal gain,
but on account of your souls' growth, particularly insomuch as to the glory of God
ye are established and rooted in the perfect
love of God, yet it is the divine will to
purge and perfect this your love for me ;
He hath shown that otherwise it would
not be pure nor cleansed from the dross of
self-love. Of a truth your love for me
were, then, indeed, a pure love if any one
of you from the time that I left you took
care to cleave more closely unto God, if
he surrendered himself entirely to His will,
being fully assured that whatever is pleasing to Him is also most fitting, and that,
not by me, but by God ye are best ruled
and directed ; unless indeed it be that,
trusting in man rather than in God, ye
have resolved to be ruled and directed by
yourselves. But if, sorrowing beyond
measure, ye so lament me absent as to
think that without me ye cannot live, then,
indeed, not yet is your love for me pure
and true, and, therefore, surely God hath
willed that I should be withdrawn from

you in order that ye may know that for the future ye must not trust in man.

I entreat you, then, my sons most beloved and most yearned after, my joy and my crown, be ye comforted, all of you, in the bowels of Christ ; strive earnestly to prevent and to surpass one another in humility and gentleness, in love, in silence and prayer, in study and contemplation. Pray unto the Lord that Himself will provide fitly for your shepherding and your ruling, nothing doubting but that of His love He will grant unto you what is best, even as He knoweth both what ye desire and what ye need, "for God is able even of these stones to raise up children unto Abraham."

But this I say unto you not because I think that I shall return unto you no more, for my longing is to see you, but in order that ye may understand wherein consisteth true and perfect love in Christ, which cleaveth unto Him alone and hopeth for aid from Him only and not from man. If ye had set before you the things which, on my departure I commended unto you, ye would not have doubted whether I should return unto you, for God Himself will fulfil the work which He hath begun, "for He stretcheth from end to end in His strength and disposeth all things pleasantly." God's affairs advance quietly, and they often suffer violence and contradiction.

Render, I beg, all of you obedience unto your prelates and superiors as unto Christ, and compare not one with another nor prefer one to another ; let there be no respect of persons with you, for "the Lord weigheth the spirits." Nay, in simplicity as unto Christ be ye subject unto all and obedient unto all, for they are His representatives, that so ye may serve God and not man. Let the more advanced amongst you and the elder in years surpass the rest in humility, and let them be an example to the younger, nor let them despise their company, knowing that the Apostles were restrained by Christ when they would keep the children from approaching Him and reproved by Him in these words, "Suffer the little children to come unto Me, for of such is the kingdom of heaven." Yet must the younger be most respectful and reverent to their elders, nor swell with pride for that they be worthy of their fellowship, but rather must they conduct themselves towards them with

veneration, modesty, silence and bashful-
ness, seldom and cautiously committing
themselves to speech. "Bear ye one
another's burdens, supporting one another";
let not any one consider the mote that is in
his brother's eye, forgetting the beam that
is in his own eye. No one of you must
speak of the faults of his neighbour nor
give ear unto the tale-bearer; judge not
thy neighbour, for the judgment of man is
uncertain and prone to error.

Whatsoever be the works of a true and
perfect love of Christ, let these works be
fulfilled in you, in order that, when I
return unto you, I may find you full of the
Holy Spirit, and it may be manifest that
ye have not been eye-servants and " I
may be comforted" and rejoice "among
you in Christ Jesus." Cease not to pray
God for myself and for Brother Basil, my
beloved son and your brother, and for the
persons here of whom I spake.

Beware of ingratitude, for it is a burning
wind that drieth up the fount of pity. I
pray you, be mindful of the benefits ye
have received of God, in particular that
He hath illuminated you and opened your
eyes, in order that ye might be able to
behold and to know the inner man, and to

F

learn that salvation standeth not in divers washings or ceremonies but in the grace of Christ Jesus and in the renewal of the Spirit, unto which salvation that man disposeth and prepareth himself who cleanseth and purifieth his heart from earthly affections, who is instant in the study of Holy Scripture and in reading, who attentively and frequently considereth the examples of the fathers, who is fervently and assiduously devoted to prayer and meditation or contemplation. For it is becoming and it is your duty to give God thanks and by your good and perfect works to praise Him, the more that He hath chosen you out and illuminated you in order to give you singular instruction in the truth and in right living. Farewell in the Lord, my most dearly beloved.

Bologna, February, 1492.

IV

To his Brethren of the Convent of S. Mark at Florence ; written on the fifth of August, 1497; concerning the manner of working in love according to the Divine disposal.

DEARLY beloved brethren in Christ, grace unto you and peace from God and from our Saviour Jesus Christ. Although now for a long time I have not saluted you by letter, it meaneth not that ye have been absent from my mind, for I have continually remembered you in my prayers ; it meaneth that we have fallen upon days of tempest when we are so occupied as to find no time for letters of consolation ; nevertheless, your instant request and my own strong desire have won from me a few brief moments. My brethren, even as in the natural world all movement is from the immovable, and an animal who would take a step forward can only do so from a firm footing, so in the spiritual world it needeth that our hearts find good foothold in the love of Jesus Christ if we would make orderly advance unto good works. Accordingly we

must believe that the root of right living is
the love of God and of our neighbour, and
believing we must strive to possess it and
to put it into operation ; and seeing that,
by the help of God, the righteous man can
everywhere and always exercise this love,
although at times he would rather be in
one place than in another ; nevertheless,
whenever it be the divine will that he be
in that particular place where obedience
to authority hath set him let him not
lament, nay, let him rejoice in life, knowing that Christ Jesus his God is everywhere, that he can serve Him and please
Him and find delight in Him, no matter
where his lot be cast.

Indeed, there is need not only that we
believe, but that we continually meditate
upon the fact that the power of God and
His providence extend to all things, even
to the very least, and that everything which
happeneth, sin excepted, is the work of
God. And because " the life of man
upon earth is warfare " we must think of
Christ as of a commander Who assigneth
to His soldiers their different posts, we
must wish to be good soldiers, to do, each
so much as in him lieth, that the war may
successfully be conducted, we must be

obedient to the commander and do our
service there where we are placed,
especially in that the commander is One
Who cannot make mistakes. When the
soldiers do not follow the orders of the
commanders, wishing to do things each
after his own fashion, then they imperil
the lives both of themselves and of the
whole army.

Accordingly in the spiritual life our
thought must ever be of exercising ourselves in love just how and where God
willeth, Who ordereth all things aright,
and hath assigned to men their different
conditions, their different merits, and their
different crowns. Wherefore in this warfare many deceive themselves, supposing
that right living consisteth either in continual prayer or in abstinence, or in study
of the Scriptures, or in other the like good
practices; and consequently, being intent
only upon one of these, they do not in all
places and at all times exercise themselves
in love, and, of necessity, they have their
special affection for particular places and
particular times. Thus it followeth that
whenever these exercises are hindered they
fall into impatience and low spirits and do
not content themselves where God hath

placed them ; they wish to rule their commander, not to be disciplined by Him; they make mutineers of themselves and often also of their comrades ; whereas, if they would but consider that right living consisteth in exercising love how and when and where God willeth ; if they would but consider that whatever happeneth unto them, whatever is given to them, whatever is commanded to them cometh from God, purposing to serve Him with a whole heart ; then would they have no regard for particular places, persons or practices, they would simply exercise love according as God hath ordained, Who useth as His instruments those to whom they are in subjection ; then would they live joyfully in the thought of the brevity of this life and the eternity of the future.

Oh, my brethren, we have much for which to render thanks to God, Who hath granted that while we are in this present life we are able to merit by exercising love at all times and in all places and under all conditions. And for this reason let not him who is weak fall into sorrow of heart, for our commander Christ hath placed him wherever he may be, in order that he may fight and exercise love with patience.

And if, weak comrade, thou sayest, " Would I were strong, then might. I do doughty deeds and be no hindrance to my fellows ! " Fool that thou art, if God hath set thee at thy post to wage spiritual warfare, why wouldest thou be wiser than He Who hath set thee there in order to discipline thee and to crown thy patience ?

See that thou amend thyself under the treatment lest thou tempt God, be content with His dealing with thee, that thus thou mayest not give hindrance unto others, but rather be unto them an occasion of merit, for they, too, should consider that they have been set at certain posts and given certain exercises by a commander Who doth not err, in order that they may practise love and thus merit eternal life. Seeing, then, that our Lord hath called you unto His service, if ye will live joyful and contented, give ye heed to peace of heart and to the exercise of the love of God and of your neighbour according to the orders of our commander Christ ; and believe me that he who doth not live thus will live a life of unrest. Nor can there be any ground for self-excuse, for, seeing that all our good consisteth in love, apart from which no good existeth and with

which all good is present ; seeing, moreover, that love can be exercised everywhere, none can reasonably say, " I am
not able to live aright here, in this office,
under these conditions." I am speaking of
persons living a duly constituted Religious
Life and of the exercises and conditions
which belong to such. Wherefore well
saith Saint John Chrysostom, " No man
suffereth injury save only from himself,"
for love which, as we have said, is our
whole good is not lost without sin, and
sin is not sin if it be not free, and accordingly none can truly suffer save only
of his own free will, none can be in trouble
save only of himself.

These things have I written unto you,
dearly beloved, to the end that ye may
consider how that the kingdom of heaven
is everywhere to be found, and that, in
order to possess it, there needeth not that
we go from one city to another, as they
do who would obtain knowledge, who go
where there is a seat of learning ; and
although it may be that we find greater
consolation from the teaching or the external worship in one place than in another,
nevertheless he who hath given his whole
heart to God findeth his consolation in

Him even in deserts and in solitudes, as we read of so many holy fathers. For the good Christian bringeth everywhere with him his own consolation, and can say with the philosopher, "All my possessions I carry in my hand."

Would ye learn that to him who hath no concern for spiritual things neither place nor condition bringeth happiness? Judas, the disciple of Christ, was a bad man, and the school of Christ was no joy to him. Nicolas, one of the seven deacons, ranking nigh unto an Apostle in the primitive Church, and many others without number, who were accounted holy, have perished. In like manner in the Old Testament it was no happiness to Ishmael that he was a son of Abraham, nor to Esau that he was a son of Isaac, nor to many others that they were of the house or school of the patriarchs or prophets.

It needeth, then, that we the rather detach ourselves from place and from condition and consider that to live aright consisteth, as we have said, in the exercise of love in every place and in every manner that our Saviour willeth. And this I say again for the sake of certain, who, when they are sorely tempted, lose heart and say that they would rather have any other form of temptation, not understanding that none can overcome temptation without the grace of God, and that by the grace of God we are able to overcome every temptation. These are they who would make spiritual warfare after their own fashion and against such foes as it pleaseth themselves ; let them consider that there is no temptation over which the godly have not won victory, and no temptation by which the careless have not fallen into sin. And thus it is that, perchance, thou shalt be overcome by the very temptation for which thou wouldest exchange that one which now oppresseth thee. Many there be who in great temptations have been victorious, while in lesser they have lost the day. David, patient and gentle under much persecution, at the sight of a woman was tempted and fell. Seek ye after God, then, my dearly beloved brethren, and have no mind for the men of this world, calling to your remembrance what saith the bride in the Canticles, " It was but a little that I passed from them, when I found Him Whom my soul loveth." Thus far have ye heard so much that it is time for you to put into practice what ye have learnt. The infant doth not always feed upon milk, but, growing in years, he eateth solid food and becometh a man and begetteth sons and daughters. And although it be that in the body ye are far removed from us, nevertheless we hold you in the bowels of our love, our brothers, our sons, our dearly beloved. Naught is there that we do not share, nay, we have all things in common, both spiritual and temporal. As for bodily fellowship it cannot in this world last for ever, and many a time doth it avail little. Had the Apostles remained always together in one place, then would they not have been able to regenerate the world by the faith of Christ. Let us, then, make every endeavour that we may be united together in that place where joy aboundeth and happiness is unending. Remember, I pray you, the sufferings of our holy father Dominic, whose feast we keep to-day, and strive to live so godly as that his sufferings and labours on our behalf may not have been in vain. Remember the word that he left with you as it were to-day, saying, " Hold fast love ; observe humility ; desire poverty." These three things if ye do then, without doubt, will all else go well with you.   If ye have need of anything ask for it, for everything that we have here is yours ; and pray for us, and we will in like manner pray for you, according to the commandment of the Apostle S. James, who saith, " Pray for one another, that ye may be saved."   The grace of our Lord Jesus Christ be with you all.   Amen.

V

To all his Brethren of the same Congregation of S. Mark ; written on the Vigil of the Assumption of the Blessed Virgin Mary, in the year 1497 ; concerning the manner of resisting temptation and of attaining unto perfection.

BROTHER Jerome, an unworthy servant of Jesus Christ, to his beloved brethren of the Congregation of S. Mark of Florence, called to the Order of Preachers, health and peace.

Having ascertained by the means of the present persecutions that your faith standeth not in the opinion of men, nor in the reason of things that are seen, but is a light freely bestowed upon you by God, which, when human reasons fail, is not extinguished, nay, rather rekindleth itself amidst tribulations, not a little rejoiced am I, and so much the more that I have, by sight and contact, full proof of your fervent desire to make advance unto perfection in the spiritual life, in that ye earnestly seek not only to observe the Evangelical Law and the Rule and Constitutions of our Order, but even to surpass

G

them, paying after the generous fashion of the Samaritan, who said unto the host, "Whatsoever thou spendest more, when I come again, I will repay thee."

I would, then, under the obligation of my office do what I can, to the end that no one of you may err by way either of excess or of defect. By the illumination vouchsafed unto me, in answer to your prayers, by Him Who giveth light unto the world, I will write of that which at the present time seemeth unto me to be salutary both for your own souls and for the welfare of the Congregation, praying your charity that ye will give such heed unto my words as not only to hear them with the ear but to fulfil them in deed. And first, dearly beloved brethren, I find that this our Congregation is like unto the temple which the Hebrew people, on their return from captivity, began to build. The foundation indeed was laid, but when there arose great contradiction many lost heart, and the work was left unfinished after such a fashion that the foundation only was complete without the superstructure. And then their enthusiasm was stirred and their zeal rekindled by Haggai and the other prophets. So, too, we have

laid the foundation of a brotherly love
which is still incomplete, the further con-
struction of which doth make but negligent
progress, and to which, by reason of continual persecution from without calling for
resistance, we have not been able duly to
exhort you.   Certainly we are not suffi-
ciently grateful to God for the light which
He hath vouchsafed to us in these days.
Being desirous, then, of yourselves to make
a beginning at the present time, let us not
be ungrateful for so great a gift, nor declare
with the prophet, "I said, Now do I begin : but the right hand of the Most High
changeth."[1]   If ye would soon arrive at
perfection in the Religious Life then must
ye, with great solicitude and with might
and main, labour at those things in regard
of which I see you to be but indifferent.
In the first place, ye ought, for your souls'
good, to believe and to hold for certain
that, so far as concerneth the intellect,
there are many wiser than yourselves,
many more fully illuminated by God than
are ye : and it needeth that in everything
ye cordially submit your own judgment to
that of your superiors, and become fools
in order that in God's sight ye may be of

[1] cf. Ps. lxxvii. 10, R.V. margin.

sound mind, as saith the Apostle : " If any man among you seemeth to be wise in this world, let him become a fool that he may be wise."

Nor must ye judge anything to be good or bad, save only as your superiors judge it to be such, for, believe me, in nothing do men deceive themselves so much as in trusting their own judgment, and he who would judge of spiritual and divine things by human reason is as one who measureth the firmament with the palm of his hand. Wherefore, in Religion it is better to become a fool in these matters, and to possess one's soul in peace, rather than to wish to search out all things and to measure them by the intellect, and to disquiet oneself where there is no need. And certain there be who, because they fell into this error and desire to measure too carefully by the intellect that which belongeth not to them, make but small profit of soul and lose many spiritual graces ; moreover, many a time doth God allow them so to err as that, in all despite, they hold fast by their own judgment ; they listen to no reason, they are confirmed in their arrogance and presumption, and lose utterly the gift of true simplicity.

So far as concerneth the will, ye know how pleasing unto God is obedience, how displeasing is disobedience, especially in the case of ourselves who have made solemn vow of obedience even unto death; no other vow do we make save only under obedience, and to obedience do we refer all things. And many do not possess the consolation and peace of the Holy Spirit for the fact that they are not ready and simple in all obedience, and that they are not in all respects, always, everywhere, and under all conditions submissive, as they should be; for they will not be like unto the ass, who alloweth himself to be driven by any one, to be kicked and ill-treated and beaten without a murmur.

So far as concerneth appetite many are sensual, and refrain not themselves from superfluities which are not essential to the health of the body, but the rather do live disorderly. And so far as concerneth anger many, too, give no heed to subdue it, nor to restrain their indignation and to curb their wrath, to which end there needeth great zeal and daily solicitude. And in effect our chief business should be to subdue and to overcome ourselves, and to hold in high esteem vile things and things which be laid upon us contrary to our natural desires, and to repress and to mortify ourselves, seeing that perfection is attained unto not by theory but by practice.

But in that what we do ourselves availeth not without the hand of God, ye must be solicitous in private prayer, and that rather briefly and frequently than at length and rarely ; yet so that, when your prayers are frequent, they may be the more earnest. Nor must ye say your Office as mere matter of habit, but compel yourselves to strict attention. And ask of God in these prayers to supply all the aforesaid needs, firmly believing that without Him ye cannot obtain, and trusting to receive from Him by His mercy, and not by your merits. Moreover, in your prayers cultivate a familiarity with God and with His saints, that so in tribulation ye may stand more firm. In the matter of external things it seemeth to me that we have many failings. And, in the first place, we are wanting in proper zeal for the due observance of the Rule and Constitutions of our Order. We must consider that he who despiseth what is least by degrees cometh to despise what is greatest ;

wherefore I would that we have such zeal
in the observance of our Rule and Constitutions, and of the ordinances which we have
received from our fathers that every least
thing be valued and observed as of high
account. And, in particular, it appeareth
to me that there is neglect of the rule of
silence, which without excuse is broken by
all in respect both of place and of time.
For, indeed, when the signal for silence is
given the brethren do not cease from incontinent conversation ; nay, they prefer
to continue talking, sometimes concerning
matters of small moment or of no moment
at all. It is the duty, therefore, of the
good Religious firmly to purpose in his
mind never to speak at forbidden places
and times, save only under the stress of
great necessity or great charity. And
should there be such stress then must he
speak with broken utterance, at least with
as few words as possible ; specially must
the superiors, although many interruptions
may occur to them at times of silence,
postpone matters, or, if this be impossible,
deal with them as briefly and as expe-
ditiously as they can. Nor must inferiors
at such times and places address themselves
to the superiors, save only under necessity,

and then with the utmost brevity and diligence. Silence is to be observed towards persons with whom speech is forbidden ; the young are not to speak in the presence of their elders, unless they are invited or permission be granted them so to do, but to stand and listen. And it were far better if, as hath been ordered by the holy fathers, there were no conversation between two or three brethren together, but rather only with due permission in the presence of the whole community, or of the superiors.

Blessed, indeed, were the state of Religion were it the custom, or failing that, were each Religious to make it for himself a custom ever to speak only what is true, to speak no evil of his neighbours, especially of any neigbour in particular ; to refrain from self-praise, from trifling, idle, worldly, angry words ; but the rather to speak gently and that of the things of God, of learning or of other matters profitable or at least not hurtful ; on all occasions to avoid grumbling, nor to listen to complaint. And in such matters the brethren ought to correct one another in gentleness and in love, and no one ought to take it ill, but the rather to thank God and his brother for a benefit done unto him. In effect, restraint of speech nourisheth, maintaineth, and augmenteth every virtue, and bringeth with it all spiritual consolation; whereas excess of speech is the enemy of the spirit, especially for the fact that it gendereth too great familiarity amongst the brethren, and familiarity gendereth mutual contempt, than which nothing is more injurious to Religion. Again, with regard to the Divine Office and the ceremonies of our Order, I observe that there is great negligence, which it needeth that we diligently amend, and that, with the utmost precision, we observe what is written, so that we may all conform in these respects to what hath been ordered by our fathers under the guidance of the Holy Spirit.

In like manner must there be diligence in study, in the which some are so indolent as to be answerable to God for lost time, and others, on the contrary, are so immersed as to neglect prayer and the due requisites of a perfect life, and to be puffed up by pride of learning. Nor must ye desire to study after your own fashion, but after the fashion of others, and ye must strive to learn and to remember what ye are taught ; and this for the glory of God and for the salvation of your neighbours, aye, and of yourselves, that so ye may not be wasting time, but by means of your learning ye may the better know both God and yourselves. The fact that there is great negligence in study is evident from the small profit that many have of it, and although they seem to be studying the year through never do they advance beyond the rudiments, nor make progress in learning.

Concerning fast and vigil, knowing as I do the bodily weakness that prevaileth in these climes, I can say little ; although I hold that such bodily weakness ariseth oftentimes from spiritnal weakness and oftentimes from an irregulated life. Indeed, were we strictly to observe the rules already laid down for us, or such rules as our superiors may in the future make with due regard to place and time —for in these matters there can be no universal and unvarying method — then would there be no excess and we should be established in good health. Nor do I think that in these climes there should be any restriction of food applicable to all alike, but the rather let each learn the measure of his own strength and guard against excess, for over-indulgence in eating or drinking doth but burden men with feebleness

and incapacity, and is the cause of accident
and of infirmity. Accordingly the Religious
must not disregard any of these least details,
albeit his chief business consisteth in subduing self and, above all things, in subduing
pride, in avoiding praise, a matter in which
many brethren are deceived by the evil
one; for, finding themselves poorly esteemed
of others, they suffer such distress of mind
as to be unable to refrain from open dis-
content. O wretched men! They have
abandoned the world in order to humble
themselves for the love of Christ, and now
have they forgotten their purpose, and in
the house of humility are they seeking after
pride! We are monks in order to be
despised of men, that so we may be exalted
of God amongst the angels. If, therefore,
we are seeking after high estate or a great
name in Religion we shall find confusion
and shame in the world to come. These
things should we study day and night, not
by the learning of books, but by the practice of the life.

Concerning works of supererogation, in
which some are forward, it seemeth to me
that generally none should be done in common save only such as the Rule and Constitutions have founded upon the Gospel,

for it is written : "He that bloweth his nose too hard draweth blood," especially seeing that, by the aid of divine grace, the observance of what we have enjoined above is very sufficient to bring every man in the briefest space to perfection of life.   But there are a few cases in which—there being at some time or another the need of being reconciled to God or of rendering to Him thanks—it might be allowed to do some work of supererogation ; as, indeed, at the present time, when we are in affliction on all sides, it were well to do something beyond our wont, to practise some special abstinence, that we may be reconciled to God.   But call to mind what saith the Holy Spirit :   "For Thou desirest no sacrifice, else would I give it Thee : but Thou delightest not in burnt offerings. The sacrifice of God is a troubled spirit : a broken and contrite heart, O God, shalt Thou not despise."   Our first duty in these days of affliction is to bewail our negligences aforesaid, firmly to purpose amendment for the future, and to fulfil in all points the pledges which we have given to God.

Accordingly it seemeth to me that in the matter of abstinence we should not at the present time practise in common any additional austerity, because we have not all an equal strength, but let each in particular do some penance of his own without ostentation and with discretion, which discretion will be best observed if he consult with the most prudent and most expert amongst us, especially with his superior, that so he may not be deceived of the evil one. And, following this fashion, let the brethren in these days put all their force into prayer ; for, where there is a good will, the purpose of a good life, and works corresponding thereto, prayer is all powerful without any common abstinence by way of supererogation, and is the more acceptable with God in proportion as it is offered with a greater humility and a deeper self-knowledge.

Believe me, my brethren, if ye will stand firm in this your faith, if ye will be humble and vile in your own sight, not seeking glory of men but taking no account of human honours and of human praise, not boasting yourselves against your adversaries when ye suffer persecution, but having compassion towards them ; if ye will persevere in prayer and in the observance of the aforesaid godly exer-

H

cises, making due use of such human means as it needeth, that ye may not tempt God, then without doubt will He grant unto you great victory, and "we shall see His wondrous works." But if ye will do otherwise, then will the Lord visit you with the rod in this present world. I well believe that to their souls' profit God will call others to this His great service.

According, my brethren, most beloved and most longed after, be instant in prayer, and have no doubt but that the Lord will grant His aid and will yet do great things for us, provided that we persevere in humility and in self-abasement, not seeking praise but the rather desiring, for love of Him, to suffer shame and persecution, rejoicing only in our election and in the glory promised to us in heaven. If, then, we obey the divine precepts God will give ear unto our prayer. Fear not ; He is the Lord, and He will fight for us ; in Him shall we gain the eternal victory, unto which may He bring us all. Amen.

Written from the Convent of S. Mark of Florence, on the Vigil of the Assumption of our Lady, Mary the Virgin, Mother of God, 1497.

Dearly beloved, the great defect is that my words are read but once, and that no further thought is given to them. They must be read frequently ; their purport must be stored in the memory : a firm resolve must be made to observe the things of which I write ; in the degree in which he hath not observed them in that degree is a man not worthy to practise any austerity of life ; for he who doth not fulfil the lesser how can he rightly fulfil the greater ?

Therefore, let this letter be read to all the brethren in community to-day or to-morrow, and in like manner also upon the Vigil or the Feast of the Nativity of our Lady, and for the third time upon the Feast of the Holy Cross, in order that thus they who know not how to read may be moved thereby, and likewise they who know how to read may bear in mind the better. The grace of Jesus be with you. Amen.

VI

An exhortation of the Reverend Father, Brother Jerome of Ferrara, of the Order of the Preaching Friars, to his Brethren; concerning the wise and convenient method of prayer.

BEING anxious, dearly beloved brethren in Christ Jesus, not only concerning your state of soul but also concerning your bodily welfare, and understanding that many of you are suffering from ill-health, especially from pain and weakness of the head, I have determined very carefully to inquire into the cause of this infirmity, which seemeth to me to be far more prevalent amongst us at the present than it hath ever been in times past. And I have concluded that this is due to the desire of wearying the mind above measure in prayer, and in meditation, of compelling it to heights unto which it cannot attain, of forcing it to concerns unto which it is not apt. Thus it cometh about that the vital forces of the spirit and the virtue of the soul are distraught and are withdrawn from their own proper functions, the brain is weakened and even the animal spirits are confounded by holy communings which are beyond measure and meditation which is forced and excessive ; hence sleeplessness and headache and many another ill, and at the last do ye become useless to the Church of God and to Religion, a burden to your own selves and to your neighbours.

Ye would pass from extreme to extreme and overstep the mean ! Consider carefully the wisdom of God in natural things and ye will see that nature never proceedeth from extreme to extreme, overstepping the mean. When nature hath many means whereby to pass, never doth she omit any one of them, but proceedeth in due order from one to another, until all be fulfilled ; very slowly and, as it were, insensibly doth she make her progress through the said means, never swerving, never staying, continually labouring from the imperfect towards the perfect until she attain unto the last perfection of the matter in hand, as we see in the fruit-trees of the orchard. When they begin to feel the warmth of spring there appear first the buds, then the leaves and flowers ; presently the flowers, as they fade, transform themselves into fruit. Afterwards the unripe fruit groweth little by little until it come unto maturity. This method, then, unto which, in the divine wisdom, nature doth conform itself, must ye observe both generally in your affairs and specially in your spiritual life.

In the first place, therefore, ye must not go from extreme to extreme overstepping the mean ; that is to say, ye must not in hot haste abandon the sins of the world and of the secular life, and soar incontinent to divine contemplation ; this is as one who would fly without wings. Nay, ye must go by the way of due means, and ye must consider that true contemplation of divine things proceedeth from perfect love, and perfect love from perfect purity of heart, which last cometh with many a cleansing and by many means. And, to begin with, must the conscience be cleansed of all mortal sin by the means of true contrition, confession and satisfaction. And afterwards, seeing that there remain many impurities in the mind by cause both of natural evil inclinations and of evil habits contracted in the world, there is need of purging out these evil inclinations and worldly habits, which purging cometh about in a long time by the means of the unwonted practice of curbing the senses and submitting them to the reason ; I say, in a long time, for I have in mind God's usual method of dealing with His servants ; I do not make of no account that which He doth outside the ordinary course, Who sometimes bestoweth in a moment the perfection of life both active and contemplative, even as upon the Apostles, to whom He granted the Holy Spirit. Accordingly, speaking of the ordinary course of the spiritual life, I say that there is need of going by the way of due means and slowly, and that perfection in the spiritual life is reached in a long time, the longer or the shorter in proportion as the grace of God aboundeth more or less, and in proportion as a man doth more or less exercise himself in good works.

And to come to something practical, let us speak, for example's sake, of the means belonging to persons in Religion. So far as concerneth external things the vow of poverty must be strictly observed ; the Religious must sooner be in want than possess anything superfluous ; he must entirely separate himself from parents and friends ; he must rid himself of all affection for them, for his fatherland and for this world. Next, so far as concerneth the flesh or the vow of chastity, he must punish his own body according to the measure of its strength ; he must mortify the bodily senses and specially the eye ; he must continually discipline the body that so evil thoughts may find no entrance to the mind ; then must he shun pride and vainglory, giving himself over to all humiliation, self-abasement and obedience, to such a degree that the heart may begin to long after contempt and persecution for the love of Christ. These are the means whereby we ought to advance ever unto greater perfection, daily purging out every ill and renewing our good purposes, above all, exercising ourselves in works of brotherly love, in patience, in spiritual reading and in unceasing prayer ; these are the means whereby a man attaineth unto a perfect hatred of self and a perfect love of Christ. And thus it is that without difficulty the mind is lifted up unto divine contemplation.

But, seeing that he who is in a state of grace possesseth, in a measure, all the virtues, he must give diligence to perfect in himself all these virtues. When, however, he is much intent upon one virtue and less

intent upon another, he cannot be giving
due diligence to the cultivation of all.
Accordingly must he strive to follow no
longer that vice to which he knoweth himself to be most prone, and to study above
everything to perfect in himself the virtue
which is contrary to such vice ; for, when
this virtue groweth all the other virtues
will grow also ; specially will they all grow,
when grace groweth which is the fount of
them all. It needeth that he thoroughly
purge the heart and perfect in himself the
virtues, and above all the virtue of humility,
that so he may be able for divine contemplation. Since, however, there is need
of constant prayer, and prayer is not
possible apart from some measure of contemplation or meditation, let a man know
that he must advance little by little, after
the manner of nature, that he must go by
the way of all due means, and neither turn
aside nor stand still. Nor must he attempt
at the first to soar into the heights of
contemplation or mental prayer, for he is
still of unstable mind and full of fantasies ;
let him the rather begin with vocal prayer
and thereby excite his mind to such devotion and attention as he may.

And, seeing that, when in this matter

we make a beginning, it is not possible for us to maintain attention for long, it is a good thing for us to pray briefly and frequently, and that with much attention and devotion ; seeing, too, that the senses move the mind, it is well for us to appeal to the eye by means of some figure, such as the crucifix or the image of Mary the Virgin or of some other saint.

Now, since Solomon saith, in the Book of Proverbs, "Give occasion to a wise man and he will increase wisdom," I will come to some particular practice. Let each brother undertake to say daily some psalm or the rosary or some prayer to his own patron saint or the Penitential Psalms, or to make use of some brief prayer that pleaseth him, and by means of which he thinketh best to move himself to devotion ; let him do this perseveringly. And when he findeth that the method he useth groweth distasteful, then, let him exchange it for another, whereby the better to excite his mind to devotion, for such is the end of vocal prayer ; thus at will its form may vary, even after the fashion of the Church, which, to the avoidance of distaste, doth duly change the offices. And if a man would pray, using neither the

Psalms nor any written form, let him pray after such fashion as followeth. First let him go before the crucifix, or, if he so will, let him dispense with any image ; next let him recollect the presence of God, knowing that God is everywhere, and let him say aloud :—

"O Lord, I know that Thou art here present with me. Thou alone dost in very deed exist, for without Thee all things are but nought. Thou upholdest heaven and earth ; Thou givest life to every creature ; Thou seest all things. Thou alone art God, Father, Son and Holy Ghost. Thou, my Saviour Jesus Christ, art very God and very man ; I thank Thee, O my Saviour, for that Thou hast by Baptism created me in Thine image and similitude amongst Thy Christian people ; I thank Thee for that, my baptismal innocence lost, Thou hast vouchsafed to pity me, and to call me and receive me into the holy state of Religion, in the which Thou hast even made me Thy servant."

Let him thus make mention, as seemeth him right, of all the benefits which he hath received of God. Then let him continue and say :—

"Lord, I have become ungrateful, times

without number have I offended against
Thy Majesty by thought, word, deed and
omission both in ignorance and in carelessness and in malice. Thou hast ever done
good unto me and I have ever done evil unto
Thee. 'What reward shall I give unto the
Lord for all the benefits that He hath done
unto me ? I will receive the cup of
salvation and call upon the name of the
Lord.' Lord, I would cleanse me of my
sins, and, with full purpose of amendment,
I renew my vows of poverty, chastity and
obedience. Moreover, I resolve to live
according to the Rule and the Constitutions of the Order and the ordinances of
my fathers ; I desire to faithfully observe
them even until death. But, seeing that
'of Thine own gift it cometh that we do
unto Thee true and laudable service,' I
beseech of Thee to vouchsafe to accept this
my sacrifice, and to grant unto me grace to
serve Thee worthily, of Thy mercy par-
doning my offences and bestowing upon me
the comfort of Thy help in time to come.
Lord, purge me of all earthly affections
and of self-love ; enlighten mine eyes that
I may know both Thee and mine own
self. I confess that it is Thou Who
workest all good in me and in every

creature ; I confess that it is I who oppose
and hinder Thee, for I am nothing ; I am
dust and ashes ; I am steeped in the
ignorance of sin, so that I am lowly and
vile in mine own sight. Teach me that
this world is but nought and passeth as a
vapour ; thus let me despise its delights and
its glory. Inflame me with love of Thyself and of heavenly things, to the end that
with a faithful and true heart, I may with
all humility serve Thee in prosperity, and
with all joyful patience in adversity, and
that I may persevere in this Thy service
unto the last."

And then must he pray for our Congregation, that God would grant unto it
increase both in merit and in number ; for
the State, for benefactors and friends ; for
the whole Church ; and, as seemeth him
fit, for others, such as relatives and those
who, standing in need thereof, have begged
his prayers ; all these must be commended
to the mercy of God.

Whenever, either for lack of time, or
under the obligation of holy obedience or
of brotherly love or of study, he would
pray more briefly, then let him begin by
making but general mention of God's
benefits and say :—

I

"Lord, I give Thee thanks for the blessings of creation, of redemption, and of the Religious Life. Pardon, I pray Thee, the sins that I, ungrateful, have committed by thought, word, deed and omission ; purge me of self-love ; enlighten mine eyes that I may know Thee ; inflame my heart that I may serve Thee only with perseverance unto the end. I commend unto Thee, O Lord, the Church and our Congregation, the State, our benefactors and others."

Or again, more briefly :—

"Lord, I give Thee thanks for all the benefits that Thou hast done unto me ; pardon, I beseech Thee, my offences ; make me Thy faithful servant even until death. I commend unto Thee the Church, the State, and all those for whom I am bound to pray."

Thus have I written, not because it is necessary always to pray after this manner and to use no other form, but the rather to illustrate a type, to give a model to each brother who would exercise himself in prayer ; these forms will serve to lead him to various other forms of prayer.

And if he will but continue such exercise with fervour of heart, then will he by degrees so far attain unto a taste for divine converse and for mental contemplation as no longer to pray audibly with the voice but to address himself to the Lord by inward recollection. Thus, at last, will he stand in need of no other model but Him " Who is blessed for evermore. Amen."

VII

A treatise of the Reverend Father, Brother Jerome of Ferrara, of the Order of the Preaching Friars, addressed to his Brethren of S. Mark upon the Feast of the Holy Cross, September, 1496; concerning the discreet and due method of the Religious Life.

THAT carefulness which the brethren show concerning their own bodily health, and which the superiors show concerning the bodily health of the inferiors, is a temptation of the evil one, who would by this means destroy little by little the Religious Life itself. The weakness and the debility of our bodies proceed, in the first place, from lack of confidence, that is to say, from the fact that we have no faith in God ; and, in the second place, they proceed from the excesses of the table. He, therefore, who shall observe that which our holy fathers have ordained concerning abstinence in the Rule and Constitution of our Order, even as it hath been expounded and applied by us, shall be of stronger spirit against temptation, and more able for good works ; he shall be more robust in body, he shall enjoy better health, he shall live a longer life. But he who shall be sensual and shall not observe this manner of life shall be the weaker both in spirit and in body, and few shall be his days. And in this matter I speak generally, for every rule admitteth of exception ; I mean not that, amongst them that shall observe this manner of life, there shall be found none that is sickly or that dieth young, but that they who shall not observe it shall be thereby the weaker and the shorter lived than they that fast. And the method of fasting is as followeth : let all the brethren who have fulfilled their twenty-first year, and are of robust and healthy body, continue their usual fast ; let those that be of younger age and those that be weak fast at least on Monday, Wednesday, and Friday, and, on other days, at supper time let them eat but bread enough to satisfy hunger and prevent *malaise*, to which they may add, at the discretion of their superior, a little fruit. As for the very young and the very feeble, let them fast, if they be in health, at least on Wednesday and Friday ; but on Monday let them sup upon bread alone,

and, on other days, namely Tuesday,
Thursday, and Saturday, let them do
as do the rest of the brethren who are of
lesser age than twenty-one years, or as
do they who have passed their twenty-
first year, but are in feeble health. They
that be sick, being unable to fast, must
fulfil that which shall be ordained by their
superior, and they, together with all the
rest, have promise of the daily benediction
of our Lord Jesus Christ and of His
gentle Mother Mary, Ever-Virgin, if they
shall diligently maintain the things which
follow : namely, first of all, a great zeal
for Religion, together with a strong desire
to do all that they can therein, and to see
others do likewise ; secondly, humility of
heart ; thirdly, silence ; fourthly, frequent
prayer ; fifthly, mutual reverence, both of
heart and of body, one for another.

The method which I commend unto
you may be confirmed by the authority
of Holy Scripture, which saith, in the
fortieth chapter of Isaiah : "The everlasting God, the Lord, the Creator of
the ends of the earth, fainteth not, neither
is weary. There is no searching of His
understanding. He giveth power to the
faint ; and to them that are not He in-

creaseth might and strength," as though, in answer to them that ask how it cometh about that our fathers were more abstinent than are we, and had better health and longer life, it would reply that they had faith in God ; and that if we, like them, had faith in God, we should be, as were they, healthy in our abstinence ; seeing that God changeth not, nor faileth, nor is weary, and although there be some that are abstinent and yet are feeble and die young, yet this followeth not by reason of their abstinence, but otherwise, by some hidden dispensation of God, Whose ways are past finding out.

Wherefore have faith in God, Who "giveth power to the faint ; and to them that are not (strong *addeth the gloss*) He increaseth might " both spiritual and bodily, and preserveth them until old age ; but the sensual and the faithless fail in body and in spirit ; thus it addeth : " Even the youths shall faint and be weary," meaning that they who live, like thoughtless boys, for self-indulgence, shall lose strength ; all the day long shall they tire themselves in their search for health, but, since they have not faith in God, although they be by nature robust, yet shall they fall into many infirmities. Wherefore it saith, "And the young men shall utterly fall"; but they that shall have faith in God, observing that which the saints have ordained, shall renew their strength, and thus it addeth, "But they that wait upon the Lord shall renew their strength; they shall mount up with wings as eagles." They shall take to themselves eagles' wings, that is to say, wings of lofty contemplation. "They shall run and not be weary," soon and readily shall they attain unto the perfection of the spiritual life. "They shall walk and not faint," they shall go from strength to strength, nor shall they fail of appearing at the gate of blessedness.

Moreover, S. Thomas saith [1] that the human body doth more often fall sick by reason of indulgence than by reason of abstinence, and quoteth Galen to the effect that "abstinence is the best of medicines," and addeth that experience evidently showeth that the abstinent live longer than do the self-indulgent. Accordingly more often is it wrongly said that lack of food is the cause of death, whereas it should be said that lack of food

[1] Sent. iv. 15, Qu. 3, Art. i. 2, (3).

doth preserve and prolong life. Seeing, then, that, provided that we fail not of our part, we receive of God every good both of spirit and of body, it seemeth to me that we ought to pray daily, as followeth : first of all, for spiritual goods ; next, for bodily health ; thirdly, for temporal goods, that, according to our poverty and necessity, God may so provide them that we be in no need of dissipating mind and body in divers anxieties, but that we give ourselves in peace to our prayers and to our studies for His honour and the salvation of our souls. Accordingly, let us pray, first, for the well-being of the whole Church, but specially for the Church and State of Florence, and say, " Hear, O Thou Shepherd of Israel," etc. Next let us beg of our Lord Jesus Christ the spiritual strength which proceedeth from the light of grace, and say, " God be merciful unto us, and bless us," etc. Then let us commit the care of our bodies to Mary the Virgin, begging of her the gift of health, and saying, " Under thy protection," etc. The care of temporal things let us entrust unto our father S. Dominic, addressing unto him the " Kind Father Dominic," etc. For protection against our enemies let us call upon the angels, saying, "Angels, Archangels, Thrones and Dominations, Principalities and Powers, Heavenly Virtues, defend us and guide us from on high." Then let there follow, "Lord, have mercy"; "Our Father"; "Remember our Congregation, O Lord"; "O Lord, save Thy servants"; "Mary, Ever-Virgin"; "Blessed Dominic, pray for us"; "Praise the Lord"; "Lord, hear our prayer"; Let us pray, "Lord of all power and might"; "Grant that we Thy servants"; "Almighty God, Who hast built Thy Church"; "O Everlasting God, Who hast ordained and constituted."

VIII

An Epistle of the Reverend Father, Brother Jerome Savonarola of Ferrara, of the Order of the Preaching Friars, to the Father, Brother Pietro Pagolo de Beccuto, of the same Order; concerning the fear of death.

MY beloved father in Christ Jesus, there is nought that I would not do to the end that the fathers may escape this infirmity, provided only that I give no offence to God. Indeed, I take all means, both here and everywhere, especially the means of continual prayer, whereby they may be freed therefrom. May the Lord grant that I be worthy to be heard of Him! It seemeth to me that surely some are too timid in the matter, and thereby give evidence of lack of faith. It needeth that they trust in the Lord rather than in their chance of escaping death. Secular persons stand in no such utter fear as some of the fathers have shown. Seeing that it belongeth unto us all once to die, he who should die of the plague [1] might well be

---

[1] This letter was written when the plague was raging in Florence and its neighbourhood.

accounted blessed, for I believe that, at
any other time, death would not find him
in so excellent disposition as at the present.
Surely there is none that, provided he be
in his right mind, ought not now to stand
ready and prepared to die, especially if he
be, like thyself, a friar or a Religious.
Our brethren here who have passed away
have taken their journey in joy, not otherwise than as it were unto a marriage feast.
Yesterday Fra Batista da Faenza earnestly
besought me that I would do him the
favour of asking the brethren to allow
him to die and to go to the heavenly
fatherland, for he assured me that it was
their fervent prayers that were keeping
him alive. And to-day we have learnt
that Frate Antonio da San Quirino, who
has had some dealings with us here, is
ill of the plague, whom we may conclude
to have brought us the contagion. We
gain nothing by flight. They, indeed,
who have charge of the plague-stricken
are all, by the grace of God, in excellent
health. This faint-heartedness which possesseth some of you seemeth to me to be
beyond reason, and unbecoming Religious,
who ought rather to desire death than to
decline it. Wherefore it doth not seem

to me that, should nothing else occur, ye ought at the present time to absent yourselves from Fiesole, nor do I hold it likely that it will be needful for any one to leave Fiesole ; should such need arise, I will give you good warning. Be ye of manly courage, that thus ye may prepare yourselves for death, whensoever it may please the Divine Will, which Will doth even now make proof of us all. The grace of our Lord be with you.

At the Convent of S. Mark of Florence, August the Eight, 1479.

K

IX

An Epistle of the Reverend Father, Brother Jerome of Ferrara, of the Order of the Preaching Friars, to certain Religious, Sisters of Santa Lena of Florence, of the Third Order of S. Dominic, and others ; concerning sound and spiritual reading.

BROTHER Jerome of Ferrara, an unworthy servant of Jesus Christ, to the Sisters of the Third Order of S. Dominic, commonly called of Santa Lena, who dwell in the Convent of S. Vincent at Florence, and to all the other Sisters and devout persons who are desirous of receiving from him letters of exhortation, grace and peace and joy in the Holy Spirit. Dearly beloved in Christ Jesus, there hath been made known unto me by your father confessor your desire of listening to my words of exhortation, or at the least of receiving from me such words by letter. I have answered unto him that I am not able at the present time to grant the former request, and that, as for the latter, it doth not seem to me to be at all necessary. Nevertheless,

for he insisteth upon this latter, that I may
in part satisfy your desire, I will lay aside
my other occupations and write something
which will meet the wishes of others also
who have made the same request as yourselves.   Ye must know, then, that the
Holy Gospel, which containeth the whole
perfection of the spiritual life, was not
written upon tables of stone or of such
like material, nor upon parchment or
paper, but upon human hearts, by the
finger and power of the Holy Spirit,
Who found the hearts of the Apostles
free from all sin and from all earthly
affection ;   moreover, by their ministry,
it was written upon the hearts of the
rest of the faithful, who by them had
been converted to the faith.   Wherefore
the Apostle S. Paul saith unto the Corin-
thians, " Ye are an epistle of Christ,
ministered by us, written not with ink,
but with the Spirit of the living God ;
not in tables of stone, but in tables that
are hearts of flesh," [1] that is to say, gentle,
tender, impressionable.   Accordingly, the
books of Christ were the Apostles and
the other saints written by the finger of
the Holy Spirit.   But, because our Saviour

[1] R.V.

knew that by reason of sin the Spirit
would be driven from the hearts of men,
and that iniquity would increase therein,
therefore, to the end that the holy doctrine written upon the hearts of the
Apostles might never fail, but be dis-
persed abroad to them that were afar
off, and preserved for them that were to
come after, being kept sound from the
corruptions of wicked men, it was His
will that the Gospel should also be committed to writing.

And, although in Holy Scripture there
be found everything which appertaineth
unto the abundance of spiritual life, nevertheless did God afterwards send the holy
doctors, who have expounded its sense,
and searched out its hidden treasures, that
so the unlearned may have profit therefrom.

But in that at the present time Christians
are given over to the study of Paganism,
many who call themselves learned do seduce
the simple and unlearned by the specious
form of vain and empty doctrine, obscuring
the truth of good Christian living ; accordingly, in order to combat this error, not
only I myself, but also many devout men
alike Religious and Secular, have set forth

divers popular treatises for unlearned persons concerning good Christian living, founded upon Holy Scripture and upon teaching of the holy Church and of the sacred doctors.

Having, then, written as followeth : *Concerning the Simplicity of the Christian Life, Concerning Charity, Concerning Humility, To Religious Persons concerning the Ten Commandments and the Rules of Perfection*, and many other works appertaining to the perfection of spiritual life, it doth not seem unto me to be necessary to write further exhortations in the vulgar tongue, nay, but superfluous, seeing that the aforesaid have been printed and published abroad, furnishing thus sufficient instruction for all who would live aright ; unless, indeed, there should arise some particular need, such as the extinction of fresh error, or the allaying of strife and discord, or the like case, by reason of which I should be bound to write somewhat according to the demands of the time and the occasion ; but again to commit to writing the same things were to become both tedious and unprofitable.

To write is one thing, to preach is

another. For the word preached is not committed to paper, and for the most part men are either of short memory or of negligent performance, and there needeth that the preacher frequently repeat the same thing to the end that both they that have forgotten may be reminded, and they that on other occasions were absent may be instructed, and they that are lukewarm may be fervent in zeal. The living voice moveth the hearer even when a man speaketh things well known and oft repeated; the thing heard differeth much from the thing read. Moreover, a thing heard told after one fashion differeth much from the same thing heard told after another fashion.

Ye, therefore, who ask that I should write unto you new exhortations, when ye have no particular need thereof, take heed that ye be not of the number of those who are ever reading and never learning, and still less doing good works. To no purpose doth he read of holy things who cleanseth not his heart after such a fashion as that the Holy Spirit may write inwardly that which he readeth outwardly, for a man doeth only the works which be written in his heart. Accordingly it

needeth that he who would have fruit
of spiritual reading and find out the true
sense of Holy Scripture, before all else
throughly purge his heart, not only of all
mortal sins, but also of all affection of self-
love, and that he read not merely to the
end that he may teach, but to the end that
he may himself attain unto good living.
And every time that he betaketh himself
to reading must he first make supplication
unto God, that as he readeth He will
reveal unto him the way of truth ; and
then must he read, with an attentive mind,
not in haste, but giving good heed unto
the sentences and committing them to
memory. Moreover, must he ever be
paying regard unto his own conscience,
even as a woman who decketh herself
turneth to the mirror, not that she may
see the things which be round about the
mirror and be all reflected therein, but
that she may see her own face and head,
lest there be aught that misbecometh
them. Thus must the soul turn to the
reading of Holy Scripture to see the face
of conscience and the head of reason, and
therein as in a mirror to consider whether
there be any disfigurement or blemish, and,
if so be, to repair the same, and to present

itself fair in the sight of the Eternal Spouse. And after that a man hath read, and hath by reading well examined himself, then must he again betake himself to prayer and beseech the Lord to pardon his shortcomings, and to grant him grace to bring to good effect that which by reading he hath learned, in order that so he may do profitable service both to himself and to his neighbours.

And he who, after such manner studieth and readeth, hath no need of many books to the end that he may edify himself. I speak of edifying self, for the doctors and they who are appointed to teach others have the duty, after that they have edified themselves in the spiritual life, of reading many other books in order to defend the truth against its enemies, and to be able the more clearly and the more effectually to instruct their fellow-men.

But at the present moment we are concerned with that reading which a man undertaketh in order to build up, and to increase, and to maintain the spiritual life in himself, in regard of which I declare unto you that he that readeth one page after the manner aforesaid, hath more profit thereby than he that readeth the whole of Scripture without feeling and without prayer.

Verily, it profited S. Anthony more to hear read those few words of our Saviour to the rich young man, "If thou wouldest be perfect, go, sell that thou hast, and give to the poor, and thou shalt have treasure in heaven : and come, follow Me," than it profiteth many great theologians to read and to ponder the whole of theology. In like manner did S. Francis have more joy when he heard read that passage of the Gospel in which our Saviour saith unto the disciples, "Nor scrip for your journey, neither two coats, neither shoes, nor yet staves," than hath he that readeth and studieth all the books in the world, if he read and doth not bring to good effect.

It needeth, then, that ye read of divine things with attention, that ye meditate upon them, that good works follow upon that which ye read. I would warn your Christian love that nothing sooner bringeth a man into evil plight than the reading and the handling of the things of God without reverence and without good works following, as experience plainly showeth. Therefore Religious persons and Secular priests,

who all day long handle divine things and
yet live ungodly, are all utterly depraved
and incorrigible, for even as he that liveth
delicately and nourisheth himself in luxury,
if he fall sick, can find no means whereby
to restore himself, so these having been
fed upon spiritual delicacies, and having
fouled themselves with the corruption of
pride and of other sins spiritual and bodily,
cannot recover themselves by the means of
preaching and of exhortation, in that it is
their settled habit to read and to hear and
to do evil works. Thus it is that they
ever hear after one fashion alone, for habit
hath become unto them nature, and such
nature they cannot change. Accordingly,
dearly beloved, ye must indeed be upon
your guard against this vice, that so ye may
not become lukewarm and hard-hearted ;
rather read little and observe that which
ye read than read much and observe
not.

We read of the saint called Paul the
Simple that, upon his asking a certain
monk to teach him a psalm, the monk
began to teach him the psalm, " I said, I
will take heed unto my ways : that I
offend not in my tongue." And, when
the saint had learnt the first verse, he

asked the meaning thereof, and the monk
answered that the meaning was this, " I
have declared and I have resolved that
I will so watch my conduct that I do not
offend against God by anything that I
say." "Then," said Paul the Simple,
" I would not learn any more now; I
would first go and do that which this
verse teacheth, and, after that will I
return to learn the rest." Several years
passed, and one day the same monk met
the saint and asked him wherefore he
had not returned to learn the rest of the
psalm. "Because," answered he, " I
have not yet brought to effect that which
the first verse teacheth." Thus it is
evident that he who would read profitably
must look to it that good works follow
upon his reading, or at least that he make
firm resolve that so it shall be.

Accordingly, dearly beloved, seeing that
ye have so many books in the vulgar
tongue, fully sufficient for the salvation,
not only of yourselves, but of the whole
world, ye must not, without due necessity,
multiply for yourselves books in the form
of letters of exhortation, but read, after the
manner aforesaid, those which ye have,
and it shall suffice you. I charge you,

then, to read these and to do the good
works according thereto, particularly to
live together in love and in humility, in
continual prayer and in holy exercises,
and to pray to God without ceasing for
us and for His own cause, that so He
may vouchsafe to open the hearts of men
to the truth and to His grace, the which
may it ever abide with you and bring you
to the kingdom of the blessed.   Amen.

X

*An Epistle of the Reverend Father, Brother
Jerome Savonarola of Ferrara, of the Order of
the Preaching Friars, to a devout lady of
Bologna ; concerning the Communion.*

DEARLY beloved, thou askest of me
that I should tell thee of the conduct
befitting a devout person who would communicate frequently ; that is to say, once a
week or once a fortnight. Accordingly,
to begin with, we must pre-suppose that
such a person be cleansed of her sins by
true contrition and full confession ; then
let it be her first concern to consider
diligently that there is nothing which is
at once more dangerous and more profitable than frequent Communion. Nothing,
I say, is more dangerous to them that
approach thereunto, the due conditions
being unfulfilled ; for such persons, as we
see and ever have both seen and proved,
become either lukewarm or vicious, results
which be specially evident in the Church
in the case of priests and friars, of whom
some are wicked and others are indifferent.
Indeed, going often unto so great a Sac-

L

rament, and that without devotion, they do but daily harden their hearts the more they make use thereof, to the extent that they become unto all spiritual sweetness hard as the very stones and utterly incorrigible.

Nothing, also, is more profitable than frequent Communion to them that approach thereunto having fulfilled the due conditions ; for we learn by experience that every man that devoutly maketh use thereof becometh daily of a better and a sweeter heart, and ever doth he perceive himself to be the more enlightened, the more humble, the more self-abased.

The reason for these two statements we are well able to adduce, but experience is a most sufficient proof, unto which all arguments to the contrary do readily give way.

It needeth, therefore, that we weigh the matter well, for therein is involved either great gain or great loss. Thou must not, then, believe, as do these lukewarm souls, that it sufficeth merely to make confession of all mortal sins ; nay, thou must bitterly bewail even thy venial sins, thou must daily renew thy purpose of good living, thou must put no trust in outward works, but

rather in inward dispositions, such as purity
of conscience, purging the same not only
of actual sins, but also even of earthly and
carnal affections—in love of God and of
thy neighbour, in readiness of will to serve
God, in humility, in patient endurance of
voluntary injuries and of grievous tribulations for the love of Christ.

Accordingly, whoso would frequently
communicate needeth to arm himself with
the thought of the danger and of the
profit which belong unto the Sacrament.
And thus armed he needeth next to purge
himself throughly by the means of contrition and confession, for this Sacrament is
the Sacrament of love, and the soul that
cometh to receive such food must be
actually excited unto devotion and love
so far as be possible unto human weakness ; and this cannot be where the soul
is occupied with worldly things.   Wherefore for such actual devotion there are
needed tranquillity and peace of mind ;
and tranquillity and peace of mind belong
only to him that giveth himself unto much
silence, unto solitude and spiritual reading,
unto meditation, unto prayer, and unto
contemplation.   Thus, then, whoso would
frequently communicate must abstain from

all harmful and unprofitable conversation ; he must compel himself to abide, so far as be possible, in solitude, in silence, and in prayer, especially upon the day before he communicateth, and in like manner upon the day of Communion : having all due care, meanwhile, that on other days the mind be not dissipated, but compelled to stay itself, so far as be possible, ever upon God ; that is to say, that it come not about that, by reason of the business in which, by human necessity, the person is occupied, prayer be neglected ; that the attention be as little as possible distracted ; that peace be maintained at home ; that abroad everything be done with wise discretion, according to the divine light vouchsafed unto him and the direction of his spiritual father.

And as for the latter he must not be of the number of the lukewarm, or the affair will not prosper ; there needeth herein a truly spiritual confessor who dealeth out of his experience with the matters of the soul, who speaketh not of what he hath heard said by others, nor of what he hath read in books ; for the lukewarm do but pervert the Scriptures and the doctors to their own ends, and experience alone is the mistress of the director's art.

In the next place, there is need to note carefully whether frequent Communion bringeth about increase of devotion and of promptitude of will to live godly, and of love towards God and towards our neighbour, especially towards our enemies and such as speak evil of us and treat us ill ; whether, moreover, the very frequency of Communion bringeth about increase of holy fear and of veneration towards so great a Sacrament, so that we ever draw nigh unto it with greater reverence and devotion. And albeit that we draw nigh with great love and with earnest desire, nevertheless, let the heart within us find itself unworthy of such a feast, being filled with confusion ; although the faith which we have in the goodness of God urge us on, let there be no confidence in our own merits, but only in the loving-kindness of the Lord Jesus.

Accordingly, if thy soul perceive that, by going frequently to so great a Sacrament, devotion and love grow and reverence abate not, then go thou frequently in all security ; but shouldst thou perceive that, by reason of excessive familiarity,

either devotion and love grow not, or
reverence abate, in such case must thou
not go so frequently. And shouldest thou
be in doubt upon these two matters, and
should thy mind fail to judge thereof
and stand uncertain betwixt fear and love,
it seemeth unto me better that love should
gain the day, and that thou shouldest make
good preparation and go, trusting in the
divine judgment ; and shouldest thou be
unable of thyself to come to a conclusion,
then submit thou to the judgment of thy confessor, provided he be a truly spiritual man.

We need to note that perseverance
costeth much toil ; many have I seen
make good beginning in the matter of
Communion who have afterwards allowed
themselves to become lukewarm, a state
of things which hath great danger ; wherefore there needeth a most constant mind,
especially seeing that our adversary
sleepeth not, and knoweth well of how
great profit it is to frequent aright so
great a Sacrament : for which reason
doth he stir up persecution against them
that communicate frequently and with
devotion, and many an one doth he
incite to make mock of them, and by
diverse persuasions to lead them astray.

Be thou, therefore, constant in observing all these things even unto death, and lend not thine ears to tongues that speak not of the Spirit.

Oxford

.A. R. MOWBRAY AND CO. LTD., CHURCH PRINTEⅠ

ImTheStory.com

Personalized Classic Books in many genre's

Unique gift for kids, partners, friends, colleagues

Customize:

- Character Names
- Upload your own front/back cover images (optional)
- Inscribe a personal message/dedication on the
  inside page (optional)

Customize many titles Including
- Alice in Wonderland
- Romeo and Juliet
- The Wizard of Oz
- A Christmas Carol
- Dracula
- Dr. Jekyll & Mr. Hyde
- And more...

CPSIA information can be obtained
at www.ICGtesting.com
Printed in the USA
LVOW01s0415050416
482202LV00028B/412/P